William Shakespeare's

Henry IV, Part I

Text by
Michael A. Modugno
(B.A., Rutgers University)
Department of English
Piscataway High School
Piscataway, New Jersey

Illustrations by
Georges LaVigne

Research & Education Association

MAXnotes® for
HENRY IV, PART I

Printed in the United States of America

Library of Congress Catalog Card Number 96-67446

International Standard Book Number 0-87891-018-2

MAXnotes® is a registered trademark of
Research & Education Association, Piscataway, New Jersey 08854

I-1

What **MAXnotes**® *Will Do for You*

This book is intended to help you absorb the essential contents and features of William Shakespeare's *Henry IV, Part I* and to help you gain a thorough understanding of the work. The book has been designed to do this more quickly and effectively than any other study guide.

For best results, this **MAXnotes** book should be used as a companion to the actual work, not instead of it. The interaction between the two will greatly benefit you.

To help you in your studies, this book presents the most up-to-date interpretations of every section of the actual work, followed by questions and fully explained answers that will enable you to analyze the material critically. The questions also will help you to test your understanding of the work and will prepare you for discussions and exams.

Meaningful illustrations are included to further enhance your understanding and enjoyment of the literary work. The illustrations are designed to place you into the mood and spirit of the work's settings.

The **MAXnotes** also include summaries, character lists, explanations of plot, and section-by-section analyses. A biography of the author and discussion of the work's historical context will help you put this literary piece into the proper perspective of what is taking place.

The use of this study guide will save you the hours of preparation time that would ordinarily be required to arrive at a complete grasp of this work of literature. You will be well prepared for classroom discussions, homework, and exams. The guidelines that are included for writing papers and reports on various topics will prepare you for any added work which may be assigned.

The **MAXnotes** will take your grades "to the max."

Dr. Max Fogiel
Program Director

Contents

Each Scene includes List of Characters, Summary, Analysis, Study Questions and Answers, and Suggested Essay Topics.

SECTION ONE

Introduction

The Life and Work of William Shakespeare

The details of William Shakespeare's life are sketchy, mostly mere surmise based upon court or other clerical records. His parents, John and Mary (Arden), were married about 1557; she was of the landed gentry, and he was a yeoman—a glover and commodities merchant. By 1568, John had risen through the ranks of town government and held the position of high bailiff, which was a position similar to mayor. William, the eldest son and the third of eight children, was born in 1564, probably on April 23, several days before his baptism on April 26 in Stratford-upon-Avon. Shakespeare is also believed to have died on the same date—April 23—in 1616.

It is believed that William attended the local grammar school in Stratford where his parents lived, and that he studied primarily Latin, rhetoric, logic, and literature. Shakespeare probably left school at age 15, which was the norm, to take a job, especially since this was the period of his father's financial difficulty. At age 18 (1582), William married Anne Hathaway, a local farmer's daughter who was eight years his senior. Their first daughter (Susanna) was born six months later (1583), and twins Judith and Hamnet were born in 1585.

Shakespeare's life can be divided into three periods: the first 20 years in Stratford, which include his schooling, early marriage, and fatherhood; the next 25 years as an actor and playwright in London; and the last five in retirement in Stratford where he enjoyed moderate wealth gained from his theatrical successes. The years linking the first two periods are marked by a lack of information about Shakespeare, and are often referred to as the "dark years."

At some point during the "dark years," Shakespeare began his career with a London theatrical company, perhaps in 1589, for he was already an actor and playwright of some note by 1592. Shakespeare apparently wrote and acted for numerous theatrical companies, including Pembroke's Men, and Strange's Men, which later became the Chamberlain's Men, with whom he remained for the rest of his career.

In 1592, the Plague closed the theaters for about two years, and Shakespeare turned to writing book-length narrative poetry. Most notable were *Venus and Adonis* and *The Rape of Lucrece*, both of which were dedicated to the Earl of Southampton, whom scholars accept as Shakespeare's friend and benefactor despite a lack of documentation. During this same period, Shakespeare was writing his sonnets, which are more likely signs of the time's fashion rather than actual love poems detailing any particular relationship. He returned to playwriting when theaters reopened in 1594, and did not continue to write poetry. His sonnets were published without his consent in 1609, shortly before his retirement.

Amid all of his success, Shakespeare suffered the loss of his only son, Hamnet, who died in 1596 at the age of 11. But Shakespeare's career continued unabated, and in London in 1599, he became one of the partners in the new Globe Theater, which was built by the Chamberlain's Men.

Shakespeare wrote very little after 1612, which was the year he completed *Henry VIII*. It was during a performance of this play in 1613 that the Globe caught fire and burned to the ground. Sometime between 1610 and 1613, Shakespeare returned to Stratford, where he owned a large house and property, to spend his remaining years with his family.

William Shakespeare died on April 23, 1616, and was buried two days later in the chancel of Holy Trinity Church, where he had been baptized exactly 52 years earlier. His literary legacy included 37 plays, 154 sonnets, and five major poems.

Incredibly, most of Shakespeare's plays had never been published in anything except pamphlet form, and were simply extant as acting scripts stored at the Globe. Theater scripts were not regarded as literary works of art, but only the basis for the performance. Plays were simply a popular form of entertainment for all layers of society in Shakespeare's time. Only the efforts of two of Shakespeare's company, John Heminges and Henry Condell, preserved his 36 plays (minus *Pericles*, the thirty-seventh).

Shakespeare's Language

Shakespeare's language can create a strong pang of intimidation, even fear, in a large number of modern-day readers. Fortunately, however, this need not be the case. All that is needed to master the art of reading Shakespeare is to practice the techniques of unraveling uncommonly-structured sentences and to become familiar with the poetic use of uncommon words. We must realize that during the 400-year span between Shakespeare's time and our own, both the way we live and speak has changed. Although most of his vocabulary is in use today, some of it is obsolete, and what may be most confusing is that some of his words are used today, but with slightly different or totally different meanings. On the stage, actors readily dissolve these language stumbling blocks. They study Shakespeare's dialogue and express it dramatically in word and in action so that its meaning is graphically enacted. If the reader studies Shakespeare's lines as an actor does, looking up and reflecting upon the meaning of unfamiliar words until real voice is discovered, he or she will suddenly experience the excitement, the depth and the sheer poetry of what these characters say.

Shakespeare's Sentences

In English, or any other language, the meaning of a sentence greatly depends upon where each word is placed in that sentence. "The child hurt the mother" and "The mother hurt the child" have opposite meanings, even though the words are the same, simply because the words are arranged differently. Because word position is so integral to English, the reader will find unfamiliar word arrangements confusing, even difficult to understand. Since Shakespeare's plays are poetic dramas, he often shifts from average word arrangements to the strikingly unusual so that the line will conform to the desired poetic rhythm. Often, too, Shakespeare employs unusual word order to afford a character his own specific style of speaking.

Today, English sentence structure follows a sequence of subject first, verb second, and an optional object third. Shakespeare, however, often places the verb before the subject, which reads, "Speaks he" rather than "He speaks." Solanio speaks with this inverted structure in *The Merchant of Venice* stating, "I should be still/ Plucking the grass to know where sits the wind" (Bevington edition, I, i, ll.17-19), while today's standard English word order would have the clause at the end of this line read, "where the wind sits." "Wind" is the subject of this clause, and "sits" is the verb. Bassanio's words in Act Two also exemplify this inversion: "And in such eyes as ours appear not faults" (II, ii, l. 184). In our normal word order, we would say, "Faults do not appear in eyes such as ours," with "faults" as the subject in both Shakespeare's word order and ours.

Inversions like these are not troublesome, but when Shakes–peare positions the predicate adjective or the object before the subject and verb, we are sometimes surprised. For example, rather than "I saw him," Shakespeare may use a structure such as "Him I saw." Similarly, "Cold the morning is" would be used for our "The morning is cold." Lady Macbeth demonstrates this inversion as she speaks of her husband: "Glamis thou art, and Cawdor, and shalt be/What thou art promised" (Macbeth, I, v, ll. 14-15). In current English word order, this quote would begin, "Thou art Glamis, and Cawdor."

In addition to inversions, Shakespeare purposefully keeps words apart that we generally keep together. To illustrate, consider Bassanio's humble admission in *The Merchant of Venice*: "I owe you much, and, like a wilful youth,/That which I owe is lost" (I, i, ll. 146-147). The phrase, "like a wilful youth," separates the regular sequence of "I owe you much" and "That which I owe is lost." To understand more clearly this type of passage, the reader could rearrange these word groups into our conventional order: I owe you much and I wasted what you gave me because I was young and impulsive. While these rearranged clauses will sound like normal English, and will be simpler to understand, they will no longer have the desired poetic rhythm, and the emphasis will now be on the wrong words.

As we read Shakespeare, we will find words that are separated by long, interruptive statements. Often subjects are separated from verbs, and verbs are separated from objects. These long interruptions can be used to give a character dimension or to add an element of suspense. For example, in *Romeo and Juliet* Benvolio describes both Romeo's moodiness and his own sensitive and thoughtful nature:

> I, measuring his affections by my own,
> Which then most sought, where most might not be found,
> Being one too many by my weary self,
> Pursu'd my humour, not pursuing his,
> And gladly shunn'd who gladly fled from me.
> (I, i, ll. 126-130)

In this passage, the subject "I" is distanced from its verb "Pursu'd." The long interruption serves to provide information which is integral to the plot. Another example, taken from *Hamlet,* is the ghost, Hamlet's father, who describes Hamlet's uncle, Claudius, as

> ...that incestuous, that adulterate beast,
> With witchcraft of his wit, with traitorous gifts—
> O wicked wit and gifts, that have the power
> So to seduce—won to his shameful lust
> The will of my most seeming virtuous queen.
> (I, v, ll. 43-47)

From this we learn that Prince Hamlet's mother is the victim of an evil seduction and deception. The delay between the subject, "beast," and the verb, "won," creates a moment of tension filled with the image of a cunning predator waiting for the right moment to spring into attack. This interruptive passage allows the play to unfold crucial information and thus to build the tension necessary to produce a riveting drama.

While at times these long delays are merely for decorative purposes, they are often used to narrate a particular situation or to enhance character development. As *Antony and Cleopatra* opens, an interruptive passage occurs in the first few lines. Although the delay is not lengthy, Philo's words vividly portray

Antony's military prowess while they also reveal the immediate concern of the drama. Antony is distracted from his career, and is now focused on Cleopatra:

> ...those goodly eyes,
> That o'er the files and musters of the war
> Have glow'd like plated Mars, now bend, now turn
> The office and devotion of their view
> Upon a tawny front.... (I, i, ll. 2-6)

Whereas Shakespeare sometimes heaps detail upon detail, his sentences are often elliptical, that is, they omit words we expect in written English sentences. In fact, we often do this in our spoken conversations. For instance, we say, "You see that?" when we really mean, "Did you see that?" Reading poetry or listening to lyrics in music conditions us to supply the omitted words and it makes us more comfortable reading this type of dialogue. Consider one passage in *The Merchant of Venice* where Antonio's friends ask him why he seems so sad and Solanio tells Antonio, "Why, then you are in love" (I, i, l. 46). When Antonio denies this, Solanio responds, "Not in love neither?" (I, i, l. 47). The word "you" is omitted but understood despite the confusing double negative.

In addition to leaving out words, Shakespeare often uses intentionally vague language, a strategy which taxes the reader's attentiveness. In *Antony and Cleopatra,* Cleopatra, upset that Antony is leaving for Rome after learning that his wife died in battle, convinces him to stay in Egypt:

> Sir, you and I must part, but that's not it:
> Sir you and I have lov'd, but there's not it;
> That you know well, something it is I would—
> O, my oblivion is a very Antony,
> And I am all forgotten.
> (I, iii, ll. 87-91, emphasis added)

In line 89, "...something it is I would" suggests that there is something that she would want to say, do, or have done. The intentional vagueness leaves us, and certainly Antony, to wonder. Though this sort of writing may appear lackadaisical for all that it leaves out, here the vagueness functions to portray Cleopatra as rhetorically sophisticated. Similarly, when asked what thing a crocodile is (meaning Antony himself who is being compared to a crocodile), Antony slyly evades the question by giving a vague reply:

> It is shap'd, sir, like itself, and it is as broad as it hath
> breadth. It is just so high as it is, and moves with it own
> organs. It lives by that which nourisheth it, and, the
> elements once out of it, it transmigrates.
> (II, vii, ll. 43-46)

This kind of evasiveness, or doubletalk, occurs often in Shakespeare's writing and requires extra patience on the part of the reader.

Shakespeare's Words

As we read Shakespeare's plays, we will encounter uncommon words. Many of these words are not in use today. As *Romeo and Juliet* opens, we notice words like "shrift" (confession) and "holidame" (a holy relic). Words like these should be explained in notes to the text. Shakespeare also employs words which we still use, though with different meaning. For example, in *The Merchant of Venice* "caskets" refer to small, decorative chests for holding jewels. However, modern readers may think of a large cask instead of the smaller, diminutive casket.

Another trouble modern readers will have with Shakespeare's English is with words that are still in use today, but which mean something different in Elizabethan use. In *The Merchant of Venice,* Shakespeare uses the word "straight" (as in "straight away") where we would say "immediately." Here, the modern reader is unlikely to carry away the wrong message, however, since the modern meaning will simply make no sense. In this case, textual notes will clarify a phrase's meaning. To cite another example, in *Romeo and Juliet,* after Mercutio dies, Romeo states that the "black fate on moe days doth depend" (emphasis added). In this case, "depend" really means "impend."

Shakespeare's Wordplay

All of Shakespeare's works exhibit his mastery of playing with language and with such variety that many people have authored entire books on this subject alone. Shakespeare's most frequently used types of wordplay are common: metaphors, similes, synecdoche and metonymy, personification, allusion, and puns. It is when Shakespeare violates the normal use of these devices, or rhetorical figures, that the language becomes confusing.

A metaphor is a comparison in which an object or idea is replaced by another object or idea with common attributes. For example, in *Macbeth* a murderer tells Macbeth that Banquo has been murdered, as directed, but that his son, Fleance, escaped, having witnessed his father's murder. Fleance, now a threat to Macbeth, is described as a serpent:

> There the grown serpent lies, the worm that's fled
> Hath nature that in time will venom breed,
> No teeth for the present. (III, iv, ll. 29-31, emphasis added)

Similes, on the other hand, compare objects or ideas while using the words "like" or "as." In *Romeo and Juliet,* Romeo tells Juliet that "Love goes toward love as schoolboys from their books" (II, ii, l. 156). Such similes often give way to more involved comparisons, "extended similes." For example, Juliet tells Romeo:

> 'Tis almost morning, I would have thee gone,
> And yet no farther than a wonton's bird,
> That lets it hop a little from his hand
> Like a poor prisoner in his twisted gyves,
> And with silken thread plucks it back again,
> So loving-jealous of his liberty.
> (II, ii, ll. 176-181, emphasis added)

An epic simile, a device borrowed from heroic poetry, is an extended simile that builds into an even more elaborate comparison. In *Macbeth,* Macbeth describes King Duncan's virtues with an angelic, celestial simile and then drives immediately into another simile that redirects us into a vision of warfare and destruction:

...Besides this Duncan
Hath borne his faculties so meek, hath been
So clear in his great office, that his virtues
Will plead like angels, trumpet-tongued, against
The deep damnation of his taking-off;
And pity, like a naked new-born babe,
Striding the blast, or heaven's cherubim, horsed
Upon the sightless couriers of the air,
Shall blow the horrid deed in every eye,
That tears shall drown the wind....
(I, vii, ll. 16-25, emphasis added)

Shakespeare employs other devices, like synecdoche and metonymy, to achieve "verbal economy," or using one or two words to express more than one thought. Synecdoche is a figure of speech using a part for the whole. An example of synecdoche is using the word boards to imply a stage. Boards are only a small part of the materials that make up a stage, however, the term boards has become a colloquial synonym for stage. Metonymy is a figure of speech using the name of one thing for that of another which it is associated. An example of metonymy is using crown to mean the king (as used in the sentence "These lands belong to the crown"). Since a crown is associated with or an attribute of the king, the word crown has become a metonymy for the king. It is important to understand that every metonymy is a synecdoche, but not every synecdoche is a metonymy. This is rule is true because a metonymy must not only be a part of the root word, making a synecdoche, but also be a unique attribute of or associated with the root word.

Synecdoche and metonymy in Shakespeare's works is often very confusing to a new student because he creates uses for words that they usually do not perform. This technique is often complicated and yet very subtle, which makes it difficult of a new student to dissect and understand. An example of these devices in one of Shakespeare's plays can be found in *The Merchant of Venice* . In warning his daughter, Jessica, to ignore the Christian revelries in the streets below, Shylock says:

Lock up my doors; and when you hear the drum
And the vile squealing of the wry-necked fife,
Clamber not you up to the casements then...
(I, v, ll. 30-32)

The phrase of importance in this quote is "the wry-necked fife." When a reader examines this phrase it does not seem to make sense; a fife is a cylinder-shaped instrument, there is no part of it that can be called a neck. The phrase then must be taken to refer to the fife-player, who has to twist his or her neck to play the fife. Fife, therefore, is a synecdoche for fife-player, much as boards is for stage. The trouble with understanding this phrase is that "vile squealing" logically refers to the sound of the fife, not the fife-player, and the reader might be led to take fife as the instrument because of the parallel reference to "drum" in the previous line. The best solution to this quandary is that Shakespeare uses the word fife to refer to both the instrument and the player. Both the player and the instrument are needed to complete the wordplay in this phrase, which, though difficult to understand to new readers, cannot be seen as a flaw since Shakespeare manages to convey two meanings with one word. This remarkable example of synecdoche illuminates Shakespeare's mastery of "verbal economy."

Shakespeare also uses vivid and imagistic wordplay through personification, in which human capacities and behaviors are attributed to inanimate objects. Bassanio, in *The Merchant of Venice*, almost speechless when Portia promises to marry him and share all her worldly wealth, states "my blood speaks to you in my veins..." (III, ii, l. 176). How deeply he must feel since even his blood can speak. Similarly, Portia, learning of the penalty that Antonio must pay for defaulting on his debt, tells Salerio, "There are some shrewd contents in yond same paper/That steals the color from Bassanio's cheek" (III, ii, ll. 243-244).

Another important facet of Shakespeare's rhetorical repertoire is his use of allusion. An allusion is a reference to another author or to an historical figure or event. Very often Shakespeare alludes to the heroes and heroines of Ovid's *Metamorphoses.* For example, in Cymbeline an entire room is decorated with images illustrating the stories from this classical work, and the heroine, Imogen, has been reading from this text. Similarly, in *Titus Andronicus* characters not only read directly from the *Metamorphoses*, but a subplot re-enacts one of the *Metamorphoses's* most famous stories, the rape and mutilation of Philomel.

Another way Shakespeare uses allusion is to drop names of mythological, historical and literary figures. In *The Taming of the Shrew*, for instance, Petruchio compares Katharina, the woman whom he is courting, to Diana (II, i, l. 55), the virgin goddess, in order to suggest that Katharina is a man-hater. At times, Shakespeare will allude to well-known figures without so much as mentioning their names. In *Twelfth Night*, for example, though the Duke and Valentine are ostensibly interested in Olivia, a rich countess, Shakespeare asks his audience to compare the Duke's emotional turmoil to the plight of Acteon, whom the goddess Diana transforms into a deer to be hunted and killed by Acteon's own dogs:

Duke: That instant was I turn'd into a hart,
And my desires, like fell and cruel hounds,
E'er since pursue me.
[...]
Valentine: But like a cloistress she will veiled walk,
And water once a day her chamber round....
(I, i, l. 20 ff.)

Shakespeare's use of puns spotlights his exceptional wit. His comedies in particular are loaded with puns, usually of a sexual nature. Puns work through the ambiguity that results when multiple senses of a word are evoked; homophones often cause this sort of ambiguity. In *Antony and Cleopatra*, Enobarbus believes "there is mettle in death" (I, ii, l. 146), meaning that there is "courage" in death; at the same time, mettle suggests the homophone metal, referring to swords made of metal causing death. In early editions of Shakespeare's work there was no distinction made between the two words. Antony puns on the word "earing," (I, ii, ll. 112-114) meaning both plowing (as in rooting out weeds) and hearing: he angrily sends away a messenger, not wishing to hear the message from his wife, Fulvia: "...O then we bring forth weeds,/

when our quick minds lie still, and our ills told us/Is as our earing." If ill-natured news is planted in one's "hearing," it will render an "earing" (harvest) of ill-natured thoughts. A particularly clever pun, also in *Antony and Cleopatra,* stands out after Antony's troops have fought Octavius's men in Egypt: "We have beat him to his camp. Run one before, /And let the queen know of our gests" (IV, viii, ll. 1-2). Here "gests" means deeds (in this case, deeds of battle); it is also a pun on "guests," as though Octavius' slain soldiers were to be guests when buried in Egypt.

One should note that Elizabethan pronunciation was in several cases different from our own. Thus, modern readers, especially Americans, will miss out on the many puns based on homophones. The textual notes will point up many of these "lost" puns, however.

Shakespeare's sexual innuendoes can be either clever or tedious depending upon the speaker and situation. The modern reader should recall that sexuality in Shakespeare's time was far more complex than in ours and that characters may refer to such things as masturbation and homosexual activity. Textual notes in some editions will point out these puns but rarely explain them. An example of a sexual pun or innuendo can be found in *The Merchant of Venice* when Portia and Nerissa are discussing Portia's past suitors using innuendo to tell of their sexual prowess:

> Portia: I pray thee, overname them, and as thou
> namest them, I will describe them, and
> according to my description level at my
> affection.
> Nerrisa: First, there is the Neapolitan prince.
> Portia: Ay, that's a colt indeed, for he doth nothing but
> talk of his horse, and he makes it a great
> appropriation to his own good parts that he can
> shoe him himself. I am much afeard my lady his
> mother played false with the smith.
> (I, ii, ll. 35-45)

The "Neapolitan prince" is given a grade of an inexperienced youth when Portia describes him as a "colt." The prince is thought to be inexperienced because he did nothing but "talk of his horse" (a pun for his penis) and his other great attributes. Portia goes on to say that the prince boasted that he could "shoe him [his horse] himself," a possible pun meaning that the prince was very proud that he could masturbate. Finally, Portia makes an attack upon the prince's mother, saying that "my lady his mother played false with the smith," a pun to say his mother must have committed adultery with a blacksmith to give birth to such a vulgar man having an obsession with "shoeing his horse."

It is worth mentioning that Shakespeare gives the reader hints when his characters might be using puns and innuendoes. In *The Merchant of Venice*, Portia's lines are given in prose when she is joking, or engaged in bawdy conversations. Later on the reader will notice that Portia's lines are rhymed in poetry, such as when she is talking in court or to Bassanio. This is Shakespeare's way of letting the reader know when Portia is jesting and when she is serious.

Shakespeare's Dramatic Verse

Finally, the reader will notice that some lines are actually rhymed verse while others are in verse without rhyme; and much of Shakespeare's drama is in prose. Shakespeare usually has his lovers speak in the language of love poetry which uses rhymed couplets. The archetypal example of this comes, of course, from *Romeo and Juliet*:

> The grey-ey'd morn smiles on the frowning night,
> Check'ring the eastern clouds with streaks of light,
> And fleckled darkness like a drunkard reels
> From forth day's path and Titan's fiery wheels.
> (II, iii, ll. 1-4)

Here it is ironic that Friar Lawrence should speak these lines since he is not the one in love. He, therefore, appears buffoonish and out of touch with reality. Shakespeare often has his characters speak in rhymed verse to let the reader know that the character is acting in jest, and vice-versa.

Perhaps the majority of Shakespeare's lines are in blank verse, a form of poetry which does not use rhyme (hence the name blank) but still employs a rhythm native to the English language, iambic pentameter, where every second syllable in a line of ten syllables receives stress. Consider the following verses from *Hamlet*, and note the accents and the lack of end-rhyme:

> The síngle ánd pecúliar lífe is bóund
> With áll the stréngth and ármor óf the mínd
> (III, iii, ll. 12-13)

The final syllable of these verses receives stress and is said to have a hard, or "strong," ending. A soft ending, also said to be "weak," receives no stress. In *The Tempest*, Shakespeare uses a soft ending to shape a verse that demonstrates through both sound (meter) and sense the capacity of the feminine to propagate:

> and thén I lóv'd thee
> And shów'd thee áll the quálitíes o' th' ísle,
> The frésh spríngs, bríne-pits, bárren pláce and fértile.
> (I, ii, ll. 338-40)

The first and third of these lines here have soft endings.

In general, Shakespeare saves blank verse for his characters of noble birth. Therefore, it is significant when his lofty characters speak in prose. Prose holds a special place in Shakespeare's dialogues; he uses it to represent the speech habits of the common people. Not only do lowly servants and common citizens speak in prose, but important, lower class figures also use this fun, at times ribald variety of speech. Though Shakespeare crafts some very ornate lines in verse, his prose can be equally daunting, for some of his characters may speechify and break into doubletalk in their attempts to show sophistication. A clever instance of this comes when the Third Citizen in Coriolanus refers to the people's paradoxical lack of power when they must elect Coriolanus as their new leader once Coriolanus has orated how he has courageously fought for them in battle:

> We have power in ourselves to do it, but it is a power that we have no power to do; for if he show us his

> wounds and tell us his deeds, we are to put our tongues into those wounds and speak for them; so, if he tell us his noble deeds, we must also tell him our noble acceptance of them. Ingratitude is monstrous, and for the multitude to be ingrateful were to make a monster of the multitude, of the which we, being members, should bring ourselves to be monstrous members.
> (II, ii, ll. 3-13)

Notice that this passage contains as many metaphors, hideous though they be, as any other passage in Shakespeare's dramatic verse.

When reading Shakespeare, paying attention to characters who suddenly break into rhymed verse, or who slip into prose after speaking in blank verse, will heighten your awareness of a character's mood and personal development. For instance, in *Antony and Cleopatra*, the famous military leader Marcus Antony usually speaks in blank verse, but also speaks in fits of prose (II, iii, ll. 43-46) once his masculinity and authority have been questioned. Similarly, in *Timon of Athens*, after the wealthy lord Timon abandons the city of Athens to live in a cave, he harangues anyone whom he encounters in prose (IV, iii, l. 331 ff.). In contrast, the reader should wonder why the bestial Caliban in *The Tempest* speaks in blank verse rather than in prose.

Implied Stage Action

When we read a Shakespearean play, we are reading a performance text. Actors interact through dialogue, but at the same time these actors cry, gesticulate, throw tantrums, pick up daggers, and compulsively wash murderous "blood" from their hands. Some of the action that takes place on stage is explicitly stated in stage directions. However, some of the stage activity is couched within the dialogue itself. Attentiveness to these cues is important as one conceives how to visualize the action. When Iago in *Othello* feigns concern for Cassio whom he himself has stabbed, he calls to the surrounding men, "Come, come:/Lend me a light" (V, i, ll. 86-87). It is almost sure that one of the actors involved will bring him a torch or lantern. In the same play, Emilia, Desdemona's maidservant, asks if she should fetch her lady's nightgown and Desdemona replies, "No, unpin me here" (IV, iii, l. 37). In Macbeth, after killing Duncan, Macbeth brings the murder weapon back with him. When he tells his wife that he cannot return to the scene and place the daggers to suggest that the king's guards murdered Duncan, she castigates him: "Infirm of purpose/Give me the daggers. The sleeping and the dead are but as pictures" (II, ii, ll. 50-52). As she exits, it is easy to visualize Lady Macbeth grabbing the daggers from her husband.

For 400 years, readers have found it greatly satisfying to work with all aspects of Shakespeare's language—the implied stage action, word choice, sentence structure, and wordplay—until all aspects come to life. Just as seeing a fine performance of a Shakespearean play is exciting, staging the play in one's own mind's eye, and revisiting lines to enrich the sense of the action, will enhance one's appreciation of Shakespeare's extraordinary literary and dramatic achievements.

Historical Background

Henry IV, Part I was most probably written in late 1596 or early 1597, and it is agreed by scholars of Shakespeare that the play was first performed not long after it was written. On February 25, 1598, it was entered in the Stationers' Register without the designation "Part I," and a quarto text of the play surfaced in 1598. In the *Palladis Tamia: Wit's Treasury* by Francis Meres, Henry IV appears in the list of Shakespeare's tragedies, and it is presumed that this reference is to "Part I."

The earliest known quarto text of the play survives only as a four-leaf fragment, and five later editions dated 1598, 1604, 1608, 1613, and 1622 have survived intact. Altogether, six quarto editions, which is an unusually large number for an Elizabethan play, are known to exist. The 1613 quarto appears to have served as a source for the Folio version of 1623. The earliest complete quarto of 1598, together with the earlier fragment, remains the most authoritative text for *Henry IV, Part I*.

Shakespeare drew the historical plot of *Henry IV, Parts I* and *II* from several accounts of English history that were written during the Elizabethan period. These histories provided many details from which he could carefully select what he needed for his plays. The primary source is Raphael Holinshed's *Chronicles of England, Scotland, and Ireland* (2nd ed. 1586-1587). In addition, Shakespeare used Samuel Daniel's narrative poem *The Civile Wars between the Two Houses of Lancaster and York* (1595) and Edward Hall's *Chronicle of the Union of the Two Noble and Illustre Famelies of Lancaster and Yorke* (1540).

Scholars agree that for the Hal/Falstaff subplot, which serves as a parallel to the major historical plot, Shakespeare may have used *The Famous Victories of Henry V*, an anonymous chronicle play surviving in manuscript which may or may not have been changed or condensed.

It has been suggested that the character of Falstaff, who dominates the subplot, was derived from several sources. One such source is probably the stock characters of Vice and the Devil from Medieval Morality plays. It is also possible that Shakespeare drew Falstaff from Sir John Old Castle, a character in *The Famous Victories.* Hal's address to Falstaff as "my old lad of the castle" in Act I, Scene ii, suggests that Falstaff may have originally been called Oldcastle, but was later renamed after the descendants of the real Sir John protested that his good name had been besmirched.

Since the seventeenth century, the question of Falstaff's relation to the main plot and the other characters has been the subject of much criticism. During that time Falstaff was believed to represent the baser qualities of man, and Hal's rejection was believed to be proper and necessary in establishing the moral intent of the author in the play. However, in the eighteenth century, the rejection of Falstaff and Hal's subsequent reformation was seen as more complex. Nicholas Rowe criticized Hal's rejection of Falstaff as inhumane and contrary to the sympathetic portrayal of the fat knight. Corbyn Morris denied the presence of a moral dilemma and considered Hal's rejection of Falstaff as Shakespeare's accommodation to the "Austerity of the Times." Samuel Johnson, however, concluded that the rejection of Falstaff was proper and necessary to establishing moral order. In the nineteenth century, William Hazlitt described Hal's rejection as emotionally disconcerting and intellectually unjustified. During the twentieth century, Hal's rejection of Falstaff has been criticized as a grievous error on

Shakespeare's part by A. C. Bradley, a Shakespearean dramatization of the "scapegoat ritual" practiced in primitive cultures by J. I. M. Stewart, and as a moral necessity by Dover Wilson.

Master List of Characters

King Henry IV—*King of England who usurped power from Richard II.*

Lord John of Lancaster—*younger son to King Henry; brother to Henry, Prince of Wales.*

Earl of Westmoreland—*nobleman; loyal member of King Henry's court.*

Sir Walter Blunt—*nobleman and loyalist to King Henry.*

Henry, Prince of Wales—*elder son to King Henry IV; called Hal by his comrades; future King of England.*

Sir John Falstaff—*friend to Hal; chief member of a gang of ruffians with whom Hal associates.*

Thomas Percy—*Earl of Worcester; brother to Henry Percy; uncle to Hotspur.*

Henry Percy—*Earl of Northumberland; father to Henry Percy (Hotspur).*

Henry Percy—*son to Henry Percy, Earl of Northumberland; called Hotspur.*

Lord Mortimer—*Edmund, Earl of March.*

Lady Mortimer—*wife to Edmund; daughter to Owen Glendower.*

Owen Glendower—*Welsh rebel; father to Lady Mortimer.*

Archibald—*Earl of Douglas; Scot captured by Hotspur.*

Sir Richard Vernon—*sympathizer to the Percy Rebellion.*

Lady Percy—*wife to Hotspur; sister to Lord Mortimer.*

Gadshill—*member of Falstaff's gang of thieves who arranges robberies.*

Poins—*a member of Falstaff's gang.*

Bardolph—*comedic member of Falstaff's gang of ruffians.*

Peto—*another gang member.*

Francis—*waiter at the Boar's Head Tavern.*

Vintner—*innkeeper at the Boar's Head Tavern.*

Mistress Quickly—*hostess at the Boar's Head Tavern.*

Archbishop of York—*Richard Scroop; member of the Percy Rebellion.*

Sir Michael—*friend to the Archbishop of York.*

Carriers—*men who deliver goods.*

Chamberlain—*employee at the inn who serves meals.*

Ostler—*manager of the inn.*

Travelers—*traders on their way to London.*

Servant—*works at Warkworth Castle in Northumberland.*

Sheriff—*searches inn for money reported stolen.*

Messenger—*men who bring news to rebels.*

Summary of the Play

King Henry IV of England cancels sending his army to the Holy Land in order to concentrate on the more serious situation in England where rebellions are occurring in Wales and Northumberland. After hearing about the valiant efforts of Hotspur, son to Henry Percy, the Earl of Northumberland, King Henry expresses his disappointment that his own son Hal is not as daring as Hotspur. To expedite matters, King Henry arranges a subsequent meeting at this council chamber.

As the serious business of war and rebellion occupy King Henry's court, Prince Hal of Wales passes his time among his friends at the Boar's Head Tavern, the local haunt of Sir John Falstaff and his gang of ruffians. After arranging a highway robbery with Falstaff, Poins, another member of the gang, enlists Hal's aid in playing a practical joke on Falstaff. Hal goes along with the practical joke, and at the same time realizes that his life as a madcap is only a temporary one.

The council meeting that was arranged by King Henry takes place at the Windsor Castle. The central issue at the meeting concerns Hotspur's denial of the prisoners he took while suppressing the rebellion in Northumberland. Hotspur explains that he did not intentionally deny the prisoners as was reported. He says that he was weary from the battle when the prisoners were demanded and, as a result, answered neglectfully. Henry adds that Hotspur's denial of prisoners is worsened since it is Hotspur who has made Henry pay ransom for Mortimer who was captured by the Welsh rebel Glendower. When Henry calls Mortimer a traitor, Hotspur vehemently defends Mortimer's actions, but King Henry does not accept Hotspur's explanation and silences Hotspur on the issue. This dismissal further incites Hotspur with respect to the King, and after several outbursts, Hotspur is calmed down by Worcester who intimates the plot to usurp Henry's power.

Meanwhile, at an innyard in Rochester, two carriers discuss the dilapidated conditions that exist in the hotel. Gadshill enters and tries to enlist the aid of the carriers and the chamberlain in his highway robbery. Subsequently, on a highway near Gad's Hill, Falstaff, Peto, and Bardolph prepare to rob the travelers who are on their way to London. As the gang prepares for the robbery, Poins and Hal plan their practical joke on Falstaff. After Falstaff and his gang rob the travelers, Poins and Hal, disguised as travelers, set upon Falstaff and his gang and rob them. Falstaff, who is left befuddled and shaken by the whole incident, runs away leaving his money behind.

While the rebellion is being plotted, Hotspur receives a letter expressing concern about the dangers involved in the scheme. Hotspur becomes annoyed at the hint that the Percys' plan may be less than successful, and Lady Percy comments on Hotspur's erratic behavior. Hotspur tells her that he cannot reveal his plans but assures her that she will soon follow him to where he goes.

After the robbery on the highway at Gad's Hill, Hal waits for Falstaff to return to the Boar's Head Tavern in Eastcheap. While he waits for Falstaff, Hal enlists the aid of Poins to play a practical joke on Francis, the wine drawer at the inn. The practical joke is interrupted by the entrance of Falstaff, Bardolph, and Peto who are visibly upset by the robbery. Next, Falstaff tells what happened to them, but exaggerates the incident in terms of the number of men who attacked them and how they defended themselves. When Hal catches Falstaff in a contradiction about the robbery, Hal reveals the whole truth. Consequently, they all have a good laugh about the incident, and Falstaff suggests that they perform an impromptu play. At the same time, the frivolity at the inn is interrupted by a message from Sir John Bracy requesting that Hal come to court in the morning. As a result, Hal's meeting with his father forms the basis for the extemporaneous play in which Falstaff and Hal rehearse what Hal might say to this father in the morning. Again, their fun is interrupted, this time by a sheriff who is investigating reports of the robbery. Hal instructs Falstaff to hide while he speaks to the sheriff, but Falstaff falls asleep. This provides another opportunity to play a joke on Falstaff as Hal searches him and keeps what he finds.

In Wales, the Percys meet to plan their rebellion and divide the kingdom they hope to gain by their insurrection. Hotspur argues about the size of the portions because he feels that his share is smaller than the other sections. After Worcester calms Hotspur's anger, the men's wives arrive to say good-bye to their husbands.

The meeting between Hal and his father takes place at the palace in London as Henry questions his son about the company he keeps. Henry tells Hal that it is not befitting for a prince to be seen with commoners. Hal acknowledges his actions and vows to take his role as prince more seriously. Henry then informs him of the seriousness of the rebellions that are occurring in England.

Once again the scene turns to the Boar's Head Tavern after the pickpocketing incident. Falstaff suggests that the clientele at the inn consist of thieves, a suggestion to which Mistress Quickly, hostess of the inn, takes offense. After she and Falstaff get into an altercation about her reputation, Hal and Poins enter marching and Falstaff joins them. Again the pickpocketing incident arises, and Hal reveals the truth to Falstaff assuring him that the money is paid back. Hal also tells Falstaff that he will lead an army of foot soldiers to aid the King's men.

In preparation for battle, the rebels meet near Shrewsbury and receive some disheartening news. Northumberland is ill and cannot meet them, Lord John of Lancaster and the King are marching to Shrewsbury, and Glendower will not be ready to join them for 14 days.

As the rebellion progresses, Falstaff regrets the condition of the army he has assembled, and the Prince and Westmoreland concur that the army is rather decrepit.

Back at the rebel camp at Shrewsbury, Worcester and Douglas advise Hotspur not to be so quick to precipitate the rebellion against the King's forces because the rebels are not as prepared as they should be; however, Hotspur rejects their advice. Sir Walter Blunt enters with an offer of pardon from the King, but Hotspur will not acquiesce to the King's conditions and tells Blunt that Worcester will be sent to Henry in the morning with the rebels' answer. The weakened condition of the rebels' plot is underscored as the Archbishop of York expresses his fear of being discovered.

At the King's camp near Shrewsbury, Worcester enters with the Percy grievances. Henry replies that Worcester isn't saying anything new, and Hal adds that he will defend the King's position. Consequently, Hal challenges Hotspur to a single fight to determine the outcome of the rebellion. Once again, the King makes his offer of pardon and strongly advises that the rebels should accept it or pay severe consequences. Back at the rebel camp, Worcester lies by telling Hotspur that the King will do battle presently and adds that Henry called the Percys traitors. Worcester does tell Hotspur about Hal's challenge, and Hotspur is eager to do battle.

The King enters the battlefield with his army, and Douglas meets Sir Walter Blunt who is disguised as the King. After they fight and Douglas kills Blunt, Hotspur tells Douglas that Blunt is not the true King. In another part of the battlefield, Douglas encounters Henry whom he thinks is another counterfeit king. Consequently, they fight and Hal intercedes to defend his father. Douglas flees and Hotspur enters. At this point, Hal and Hotspur engage in single combat, and Hal kills Hotspur. Meanwhile, Douglas reenters and fights with Falstaff who feigns death. Douglas flees again, and Hal stumbles upon the fallen Falstaff whom he believes to be dead. After Hal leaves, Falstaff gets up, sees Hotspur dead, fears Hotspur's faking death too, and stabs him in the leg. When Hal enters, he sees Falstaff carrying Hotspur on his back, and Falstaff says that he killed Hotspur. Of course, Hal knows this to be a lie, but goes along with Falstaff's story to the amusement of all. King Henry, the Prince of Wales, and Lord John of Lancaster enter with Worcester and Vernon as prisoners. King Henry denounces Worcester's actions and sentences both Worcester and Vernon to death. Hal lets the King know that Douglas has been taken, and Henry relegates Douglas' fate to Hal, who in turn tells his brother John to determine Douglas' fate. Finally, the King divides the remaining powers to suppress the other rebellions.

Estimated Reading Time

If a text with ample footnotes is used, an average student should be able to read each act in an hour when reading the play for the first time. Subsequent readings should take less time as familiarity with the story, characters, and language increases. It is suggested that an entire act or a few scenes be read in one sitting. Since there are five acts with a total of 19 scenes, the student could expect to complete the play in at least five hours, or five to seven sessions.

SECTION TWO

Act I

Act I, Scene 1

New Characters:

King Henry IV: *King of England; seized power from Richard II*

Lord John of Lancaster: *younger son to King Henry IV*

Earl of Westmoreland: *nobleman; loyalist to King Henry IV*

Sir Walter Blunt: *nobleman; loyalist to Henry IV*

Summary

At the King's palace in London, Henry expresses deep concern about the current rebellions in England and vows to stop all wars. As he promised when he became King, he sends an army to fight the Crusades to fulfill his vow. He asks Westmoreland what the council decreed regarding the matter of the Crusades, and Westmoreland replies that the issue was undergoing serious discussion when they received news from Wales that Mortimer, a nobleman, had been taken by Glendower, a Welsh rebel. In addition, thousands of Welsh were butchered, and Welshwomen performed atrocities on the corpses. This news causes Henry to cancel his army to the Holy Land to concentrate on stopping the rebellions at home. Westmoreland adds that on September 14, Hotspur engaged in a battle at Holmedon with Archibald, Earl of Douglas.

Sir Walter Blunt brings the good news that the Earl of Douglas is taken, and that Blunt saw 10,000 Scots and 22 knights bathed in their own blood. He adds that Hotspur took Mordake, Earl of Fife and Douglas' eldest son, Earls of Athol, Murray, Angus, and Menteith as prisoners. At this news, King Henry is disappointed that his own son Henry is not as valiant as Hotspur. Henry asserts that Hotspur has made it clear that he will keep for his own use all of the prisoners he has taken except Mordake, Earl of Fife. Westmoreland tells the King that Worcester, Hotspur's uncle, is responsible for Hotspur's arrogance. The King cancels the army to Jerusalem and arranges a council meeting for the following Wednesday at Windsor.

Analysis

Henry's opening line, "So shaken as we are, so wan with care," establishes the chaotic atmosphere in which the actions of the play take place. He speaks of "frighted peace" that can scarcely catch its breath before it has to "breathe short-winded accents of new broils" on England's shores. The personification continues as he vows, "No more the thirsty entrance of this soil / Shall daub her lips with her own children's blood," suggesting an image of England as a depraved mother detroying her own children rather than nurturing them. He adds that "No more shall trenching war channel her fields, / Nor bruise her flow'rets," speaking as a king whose aim is to protect the motherland rather than to witness its destruction. The conditions of "civil butchery" must not be allowed to prevail as the "edge of war, like an ill-sheated knife, / No more shall cut his master."

To reinforce the graphic imagery of civil wars that rend the country to its foundations, Westmoreland tells Henry that "the noble Mortimer" was taken, "a thousand of his people butchered," and that to the corpses "there was such misuse, / Such beastly shameless transformation, / By those Welshwomen done." In the north, Hotspur spent a "sad and bloody hour" fighting Archibald, Earl of Douglas, and the King adds that Sir Walter Blunt saw "ten thousand bold Scots...Balked in their own blood."

When Henry hears about the conquests of Hotspur, he expresses his disappointment that his own son Henry is not as valiant as Hotspur. He suggests that perhaps "some night-tripping fairy had exchanged / In cradle clothes" his son Henry for Henry Percy's son Hotspur when they were babies. The issue of Hal's loose behavior provides the basis for the subplot that develops. The opening scene of the play establishes the chaotic world of Henry's court where he attempts to restore order.

Act I, Scene 2

New Characters:

Henry: *Prince of Wales; also known as Hal among his friends*

Sir John Falstaff: *friend to Hal; chief member of the band of thieves*

Poins: *a member of Falstaff's gang of ruffians*

Summary

This scene takes place at the prince's lodging at a London inn. The prince and Falstaff enter and engage in a humorous conversation about Falstaff's excessive drinking and his reputation as a thief. Falstaff teases Hal by saying that when Hal becomes king, highwaymen should be considered noble and not be hanged. In return, Hal jokes and tells Falstaff that when he is king, he will appoint Falstaff as hangman to thieves. After their joking, Poins enters with news that in the morning at Gad's Hill pilgrims will be traveling to Canterbury and traders will be riding to London. Poins and Falstaff agree that the travelers are an excellent group to rob. Then Poins tells Hal he has a joke to play on Falstaff. After Falstaff, Bardolph, Peto, and Gadshill rob the travelers, Hal and Poins will disguise themselves as highwaymen and rob Falstaff and his gang. To go along with the joke, Hal agrees to participate in the "robbery" of Falstaff and the gang. At the end of the scene he expresses his thoughts about his madcap life and says he will prove his true worth as the King's son when he is called upon to do so.

Analysis

Prince Hal, whose favorite haunt is the tavern world of London, teases Falstaff about being "so fat-witted with drinking of old

sack." Hal's description of Falstaff as being "fat," literally because of his rotund size, and "witted" because of his tendency to engage in verbal humor aptly creates an impression of Falstaff that is sustained throughout the play. This scene, with its tavern setting and humorous atmosphere, contrasts the seriousness of the previous scene. In addition, this scene establishes the world of Falstaff and his band of ruffians who provide comic relief from the dramatic events of King Henry's world of war. Falstaff, likewise, teases that when Hal is king he should "let men say we be men of good government, being governed by...our noble and chaste mistress the moon under whose countenance we steal." Falstaff uses the pun on the word steal, for as robbers they steal valuables while they steal about under the light of the moon. In another tête-a-tête, Falstaff mocks "were it not here apparent that thou art heir apparent" to tease Hal about how much he uses his credit. Falstaff implies that if it were not "here apparent" at the inn that Hal is the "heir apparent," inheritor of the crown, his credit would be overextended. This type of verbal banter between the two men contrasts the serious nature of the talk of war.

However, much of the comic dialogue provides commentary on the chaotic conditions of the world apart from the battlefield. Poins' suggestion of "a jest to execute" on Falstaff gives Hal the chance to "be a madcap" one more time before he, too, must

engage in the serious business of war. At the end of the scene, Hal's soliloquy reveals that he "will awhile uphold / The unyoked humor" among his friends, but that "herein will I imitate the sun" when the occasion should arise. Here Hal's use of the pun on the word sun suggests the more serious side of the play. As the sun reveals itself from behind dark clouds, so will the son of the King reveal himself from among the questionable company he keeps when "this loose behavior" Hal throws off.

Act I, Scene 3

New Characters:

Thomas Percy: *Earl of Worcester; brother to Henry Percy; uncle to Hotspur*

Henry Percy: *Earl of Northumberland; father to Henry Percy (Hotspur)*

Henry Percy: *son to Henry Percy, Earl of Northumberland; also known as Hotspur*

Summary

As arranged by Henry in a previous scene, a meeting regarding Hotspur's denial of prisoners takes place at Windsor in the council chamber. King Henry IV, Earl of Northumberland, Earl of Worcester, Hotspur, and Sir Walter Blunt are present. King Henry is determined to be harsh in his dealings with the Percy family and those who may rebel against him. Worcester's reminder to the King that his own position was obtained with the Percys' help causes Henry to dismiss Worcester. Northumberland defends his son by saying that Hotspur denied no prisoners. Hotspur then says that he denied no prisoners but answered neglectfully when the King's man demanded the turnover of Hotspur's prisoners. Blunt adds that the matter should be dropped; however, Henry pursues the issue by stating that Hotspur will deny his prisoners until Henry ransoms Mortimer, whom he considers to be a traitor. At this, Hotspur defends Mortimer's actions, but Henry accuses him of misrepresenting Mortimer. Finally, Henry stops all talk of Mortimer and demands Hotspur's prisoners.

When the King leaves, Hotspur repeatedly displays his anger at being silenced about Mortimer. Next, he begins a series of speeches in which he criticizes Henry for mistreating the Percy family, who helped Henry gain his power as king. Finally, Worcester calms Hotspur down by intimating the rebel plot to usurp King Henry's power.

Analysis

The council meeting at Windsor reveals the side of King Henry which is prepared to be "mighty and to be feared" in dealing with "these indignities" he has suffered at the Percys' hands. King Henry's assertion of the need to "rather be myself" echoes Prince Hal's recognition that he, too, will "please again to be himself" in the previous scene. Henry follows his words with action when he says to Worcester, "get thee gone, for I do see / Danger and disobedience in thine eye," after Worcester reminded Henry of the Percys' help in obtaining his crown. In addition, Henry maintains an adamant approach in dealing with the issue of Hotspur's prisoners.

This scene also reveals the side of Hotspur with which not only King Henry must deal, but also the other rebels as well. At Henry's accusation that he denied prisoners, Hotspur strongly asserts "I did deny no prisoners" and proceeds to tell of the circumstances under which he gave his response when the prisoners were demanded. Hotspur says that he was weary with war when "there came a certain lord, neat and trimly dressed...chin newly reaped... perfumed like a milliner" who spoke "with many holiday and lady terms...so like a waiting gentlewoman" as he demanded prisoners. Hotspur recollects how the gentleman's speech, outward appearance, and condescending attitude toward battle created such an incongruity on the battlefield that it caused him to answer neglectfully when asked to release the prisoners. This account also reveals Hotspur's perception of a man's role in his world "Of guns and drums and wounds." Even the iambic rhythm of this line, with its trio of stresses on the words guns, drums, and wounds, imitates the images of war that march across the battlefield. When Henry refuses to meet Hotspur's request to

"ransom straight / His brother-in-law, the foolish Mortimer… revolted Mortimer," Hotspur forcefully defends Mortimer's actions in the battle with Owen Glendower.

After Henry accuses Hotspur of lying about the encounter, Hotspur becomes more incensed. Finally, Henry demands that Hotspur not "speak of Mortimer" and that Hotspur send his "prisoners with the speediest means." Consequently, Hotspur's anger increases. As Worcester and Northumberland try to calm Hotspur down, they recognize that his anger is justified because Mortimer was proclaimed heir to the throne by Richard II. Hotspur is angered that after the Percys helped Henry IV regain his dukedom of Lancaster. Henry deposed Richard II, thereby implicating the Percys in a conspiracy and depriving them of their claim to the throne.

At the center of Hotspur's motivations is the redemption of the

Percys' lost honor. Hotspur believes "yet time serves wherein [the Percys] may redeem / [their] banished honors and restore [themselves]." In addition, for Hotspur "it were an easy leap / To pluck bright honor from the pale-faced moon...So he that doth redeem her might" reclaim honor without sharing it. At this point, Hotspur is open to Worcester's hint of rebellion, and the scene ends with Hotspur eager for the time "Till fields and blows and groans applaud our sport." The iambic rhythm of this line repeats the three word stress of Hotspur's previous statement "of guns and drums and wounds" used with reference to "a certain lord" who asked for the prisoners.

Study Questions

1. What are King Henry's concerns at the opening of Act I?
2. What news does Westmoreland bring to King Henry regarding the political state of affairs in England?
3. Explain Henry's disappointment in his son Hal.
4. Describe the relationship between Hal and Falstaff.
5. Explain the joke that Poins plans to play on Falstaff with the help of Hal.
6. What does Hal reveal about his position as Prince of Wales and the company of friends he keeps?
7. Explain King Henry's reaction to Worcester at the opening of Scene iii.
8. What defense does Hotspur offer on his own behalf with respect to the accusation that he denied prisoners?
9. Why does Hotspur become so angry when Henry refuses to pay ransom for Mortimer?
10. How do Northumberland and Worcester calm Hotspur down at the end of Scene iii?

Answers

1. King Henry's concerns involve sending an army to the Holy Land to fight in the Crusades and suppressing rebellions that

are occurring in England. It is no surprise that at the beginning of the play we meet a king "so shaken" and "wan with care" because of his concern for his kingdom.

2. Westmoreland brings Henry news that the issue of an army to the Crusades was being heavily discussed when news came that "the noble Mortimer, / Leading the men of Herefordshire to fight" against Glendower was taken by Glendower. He adds that thousands of people were butchered in the fight, and Welshwomen performed "shameless transformation" upon the corpses. Also, in Scotland, Hotspur succeeded in taking "that ever-valiant, and approved Scot," Archibald, Earl of Douglas.

3. After Henry hears of Hotspur's valiant efforts, King Henry is disappointed that he sees "riot and dishonor" in his son Hal. The discrepancy between Hotspur's action and Hal's inaction on the field give Henry cause to wonder if "some night-tripping fairy had exchanged" his son for Hal when they were babies.

4. Hal and Falstaff share a relationship of mutual affection that is demonstrated through the constant matching of verbal wits. Hal's disparaging remarks to Falstaff with respect to his drinking and his weight are countered by Falstaff's taunts about Hal's inexperience and naiveté.

5. Poins wants to play a practical joke on Falstaff in which he and Hal disguise themselves as thieves and then pretend to rob Falstaff after he and the rest of the gang rob the travelers on the road near Gad's Hill.

6. In his soliloquy at the end of Scene ii, Hal recognizes that his madcap adventures are temporary and must end some day, as he will "imitate the sun." With this play on the word sun, Hal suggests that, like the sun which often appears from behind dark clouds, he will some day appear from behind the common side of life to prove himself as the King's son "redeeming time when men think least" that he will.

7. The King distrusts Worcester because of the "danger and disobedience" he sees in Worcester's eyes. Henry is also im-

patient with "these indignites" on behalf of the Percys, so he dismisses Worcester until he is needed.

8. When King Henry accuses Hotspur of denying prisoners, Hotspur defends his actions by stating that he did not intentionally deny the prisoners. He tells of how battle weary he was when someone from the court demanded the prisoners. The "certain lord" who was "perfumed like a milliner" and spoke "with many holiday and lady terms" offended Hotspur, so in his disgust he answered neglectfully.
9. Henry believes that Mortimer voluntarily joined the rebel forces, so he calls Mortimer a traitor. This angers Hotspur who believes that Mortimer "never did fall off" and continues to describe the fierce battle Mortimer waged with Glendower.
10. Northumberland and Worcester calm Hotspur down by intimating that the rebellion which is "ruminated, plotted, and set down" only needs a single occasion to bring it to fruition.

Suggested Essay Topics

1. Explain how the alternating scenes at the King's palace in London, the Prince's lodging at the inn, and the council chamber at Windsor castle establish the main plot and subplot of the play.
2. Describe Falstaff in terms of his physical traits and his personality.

SECTION THREE

Act II

Act II, Scene 1

New Characters:

Carriers: *men who deliver goods*

Gadshill: *member of Falstaff's gang of thieves; arranges robberies*

Chamberlain: *inn employee who serves meals*

Ostler: *manager of the inn*

Summary

At 4:00 in the morning at an innyard in Rochester, a carrier enters and discusses with a second carrier the chaotic conditions that prevail at the inn. Both men are impatient since the ostler has not prepared their horses with which they are to deliver their goods. Gadshill enters and tries to find out what time the carriers will arrive in London. He then calls a chamberlain who informs him that a rich farmer who is at the inn will be leaving presently. Gadshill asks the chamberlain if he wants to go along with the robbery, but the chamberlain refuses.

Analysis

This scene provides a glimpse of the run down conditions that prevail at the inn, which "is turned upside down since Robin Ostler died." The carrier's implication that the new ostler has been

remiss in his duties is supported by the statement that his horse's saddle be softened and the pommel be padded because the horse "is wrung in the withers out of all cess." The horse is excessively worn and raw at the shoulders due to a lack of care as is most of Henry's kingdom. Next, the second carrier's comment that "peas and beans are as dank here as a dog" suggests the rampant decay. Furthermore, the inn is "the most villainous house in all London road for fleas." Corruption can be seen in everyone from Gadshill who arranges highway robberies to the chamberlain who varies "no more from picking of purses than giving direction doth from laboring."

Ironically, Gadshill distinguishes himself from the common lot of thieves, "footland robbers" and "long-staff six penny strikers," and drunks, "mad mustachio purple-hued maltworms," when he says his type of thieving is joined with nobility and tranquility. His entire outlook on the world is as topsy-turvy as the situation at the inn. The laid back atmosphere and the dilapidated conditions of the inn mirror the chaos that exists in England.

Act II, Scene 2

New Characters:

Bardolph: *a member of Falstaff's gang of thieves*

Peto: *another member of the gang*

Travelers: *traders on their way to London*

Summary

This scene begins on the highway near Gad's Hill, a place in Rochester near Kent that was notorious for the many highway robberies that occurred there. Falstaff enters befuddled because he cannot find his horse, so he calls Poins. Hal enters and tells Falstaff that Poins has walked up the hill and that he himself will go get Poins. Falstaff is anxious to get on with the plan and calls his friends, Bardolph and Peto. Hal reenters and tells Falstaff to lie down with his ear to the ground to listen for the sounds of travelers. Gadshill and Bardolph enter with masks to use as disguises. Next, Hal instructs Falstaff and the rest of the gang to take their places in a narrow lane in order to rob the travelers while he and Poins wait in another location should the travelers elude Falstaff. Just before Hal and Poins leave, they put on their masks. The travelers enter, and Falstaff and the others rob the travelers and bind them. While Falstaff and his men share the booty, Hal and Poins, disguised as thieves, approach them. All flee except Falstaff, who ineffectively throws a few blows in the air in an attempt to defend himself. Finally, he runs, leaving the money behind.

Analysis

Falstaff's nature is presented in this comic scene as he deals with the practical joke played on him by Poins and Hal. When

Falstaff enters, he complains that his horse is not available and that he is too tired to walk. He suggests that he was enticed into Poins' company by some medicines so he is "bewitched with the rogue's company" even though he has tried to break away for 22 years. Falstaff will not admit to himself that he steals because he likes to do it. As a result, he implies that Poins and the others need him as their comrade because he is "the veriest varlet that ever chewed with a tooth," and he exaggerates his own importance among his friends.

After Hal enters, the verbal bantering between the two begins as Hal calls Falstaff "ye fat-guts!" and tells him to lie down with his ear to the ground to listen for travelers. Falstaff's reference to his own size is clear when he responds to Hal by asking, "Have you any levers to lift me up again?" After Falstaff and his gang rob the travelers, Falstaff suggests they share the money, and he calls Hal and Poins "two arrant cowards" and says there is "no more valor in Poins than in a wild duck." However, when Falstaff is set upon by Hal and Poins, he exhibits his own brand of cowardice and lack of valor as he fruitlessly defends himself by throwing a few blows in the air and running away without the money.

Act II, Scene 3

New Characters:

Lady Percy: *wife to Hotspur; sister to Lord Mortimer*

Servant: *interupts Lady Percy and Hotspur's conversation*

Summary

At Warkworth Castle in Northumberland, Hotspur reads a letter from one of the rebels who expresses his doubts about the viability of the plot to usurp Henry. Hotspur shows his contempt for the rebel. Lady Percy, Hotspur's wife, then enters and comments on Hotspur's loss of appetite, nervousness, and lack of interest in her. A servant interrupts their conversation with news that Hotspur's horse is ready. When Lady Percy asks Hotspur what takes him away from home, he tells her that he must keep it a secret.

Analysis

The interaction between Hotspur and Lady Percy provides more insight into Hotspur's nature. When he reads the letter suggesting the dangerous nature of the rebellion, he responds by stating that the letter writer is "a sallow, cowardly hind," "a lack brain," and "a frosty spirited rogue" whom he "could brain with his lady's fan" because the man is "such a dish of skim milk." To Hotspur, a man who does not demonstrate an eagerness to fight does not measure up to the image of a real man. This attitude is also evident in his perception of "a certain lord" who demanded the prisoners on the battlefield in a previous scene. Lady Percy observes that lately, in his sleep, Hotspur speaks of "sallies and retires, of trenches, tents / Of pallisadoes, frontiers, parapets / Of Basilisks, of cannon and culverin." Hotspur is preoccupied with war, almost to the point of obsession.

Their conversation takes on a lighter tone after the servant tells Hotspur his horse is ready. When Lady Percy asks, "What is it carries you away?", Hotspur answers teasingly, "Why, my horse, my love—my horse!" Hotspur again expresses his view of a man's role when he says, "This is no world / To play with mammets and to tilt with lips. / We must have bloody noses and cracked crowns." In the man's world, Hotspur has no time for girlish games with dolls and clever talk. To Hotspur, the measure of a man is his ability to fight. However, the scene does show the affectionate side of Hotspur who tells Lady Percy, "Wither I go, thither shall you go too."

Act II, Scene 4

New Characters:

Francis: *apprentice wine drawer (waiter) at the Boar's Head Tavern in Eastcheap*

Vintner: *innkeeper at the Boar's Head Tavern*

Mistress Quickly: *hostess at the Boar's Head Tavern*

Sheriff: *arrives to search the inn for stolen money*

Summary

In the Boar's Head Tavern in the Eastcheap section of London, Hal enlists the aid of Poins in playing a joke on Francis, the apprentice drawer. While Hal talks to Francis about his apprenticeship as a waiter, Poins interrupts the conversation by calling Francis' name, to which Francis responds "Anon." As the conversation proceeds, so does Poins' insistence until Francis is amazed, not knowing which way to go. The vintner finally stops the joke when he orders Francis to attend to the guests at the inn.

Falstaff, Gadshill, Bardolph, and Peto enter, and Hal inquires about Falstaff's bristly mood. Falstaff then proceeds to tell how he and the others were robbed earlier in the day. As he tells the story he exaggerates about the number of men who attacked him and the degree of struggle he maintained with them. Hal goads Falstaff with questions about the robbery until he catches Falstaff in a contradiction about the details of the assault. Hal finally tells Falstaff that he and Poins were the "thieves." Falstaff tries to get himself out of an embarrassing situation by saying that he knew that all along Hal and Poins had robbed him. At this point they all laugh, and Falstaff suggests they perform an impromptu play. Mistress Quickly, hostess at the tavern, enters and tells Hal that a gentleman from the court wishes to speak with him. Falstaff tells her he will send the gentleman away. When Falstaff returns, he tells Hal that Sir John Bracy's message is for Hal to appear in the court in the morning because of the rebellions that are brewing.

After the interruption, Falstaff and Hal resume their impromptu play, in which they rehearse what Hal might say to his father the next morning at the court. Falstaff plays King Henry, and Hal plays himself. A knocking at the door interrupts their fun, and a sheriff comes to search the inn for the money that two gentlemen reported as stolen. Hal assures the sheriff that he will assist with the investigation, and when the sheriff leaves, Hal searches Falstaff's pockets, but keeps the contents.

Analysis

Once again, the seriousness "of guns and drums and wounds" is replaced by the comic relief in the life at the Boar's Head Inn. The opening incident illustrates that Hal is as quick to create humor

"to drive away the time till Falstaff come" as any one of his cronies is when he plays a practical joke on Francis, the waiter at the inn. The lighthearted joke on Francis also provides a glimpse into the working class world of Elizabethan England.

After the joke with Francis, Hal contemplates for a moment the difference between Hotspur and himself. He creates a mock conversation between Hotspur, who kills "some six or seven dozen of Scots at a breakfast," and Lady Hotspur, who asks "How many hast thou killed today?" This scenario prompts him to create an extemporaneous dialogue between Falstaff and himself in an attempt to give his serious thought some levity.

However, Falstaff enters and is disturbed because he was robbed earlier. At the core of his distraction is "the roguery to be found in villainous man" as he calls his friends cowards because they ran and left him to be robbed. His bombastic speech about cowardice is ironic because he is not aware that Hal and Poins know exactly what happened. Falstaff begins to tell how he "scaped by a miracle" when he was robbed. As the story progresses, Falstaff embellishes the number of his attackers and the way he "valiantly" fought them off. Finally, he gets so carried away with his story that Hal catches him in a contradition. Falstaff says, "three misbegotten knaves in Kendal green" came at his back when it was so dark "that thou couldst not see thy hand." Hal catches him in the lie and responds with "These lies are like their father that begets them—gross as a mountain, open, palpable." When Hal tells Falstaff that he and Poins were the ones who attacked him, Falstaff tries to get out of his lie by saying, "I knew ye as well as he that make ye" to claim he was "a coward on instinct" so as not to harm Hal.

To continue the levity, Falstaff suggests "a play extempore." At this point, Mistress Quickly's news that "a nobleman of the court at the door" wishes to speak with Hal prompts Falstaff to leave and return with the message that Hal "must to the court in the morning." Falstaff informs Hal of the serious Percy Rebellion which provides the basis for the "play extempore" that was interrupted.

This scene between Falstaff and Hal is a key scene because it represents the point at which the world of the battlefield touches Hal's world of the inn and forces Hal to begin facing his responsibilities. In the impromptu play, Falstaff and Hal rehearse what Hal might say to his father in the morning. In a comic scene with more serious suggestions, Falstaff takes on the role of King Henry and Hal plays himself. The focus of the conversation is the King's confrontation of Hal about the company he keeps. In the scene, Falstaff admonishes his "son" for the type of friends he has, but points out that even among his cronies "there is a virtuous man." The reference to himself allows Falstaff the chance to itemize his many virtues until Hal stops him and they reverse roles. As the King, Hal takes his opportunity to admonish his "son" for falling from grace because "There is a devil haunts thee in the likeness of an old fat man." Hal proceeds to recite a series of epithets that point out Falstaff's gross size and drunkenness. At that, Hal's tone changes from a comic one to a more serious and biting tone. Consequently, Falstaff says, "take me with you" because he detects more intent in

Hal's speech. By this time, the extemporaneous aspect of their dialogue has lost its effect, and Hal's tone prompts Falstaff to defend himself and say "Banish not him." It is as if Falstaff senses the beginning of the end of their friendship and makes a desperate plea to remain one of Hal's friends.

The hostess' announcement that the sheriff has arrived to search the inn breaks the serious tone that has developed between Hal and Falstaff. By the end of this scene, Hal's reformation has begun as a result of his awareness of Hotspur's actions and his own responsibilities as future king.

Study Questions

1. Describe the conditions that exist at the inn at Rochester.
2. How do Poins and Hal set Falstaff up for their practical joke?
3. Explain how Falstaff deals with the "thieves" who rob him.
4. What do Hotspur's comments about the letter writer reveal about his nature?
5. What observation does Lady Percy make regarding Hotspur's recent behavior?

6. How does Hal display his ability to create a practical joke?
7. Describe Falstaff's temperament when he arrives at the tavern in Eastcheap.
8. How does Falstaff's description of the robbery contrast to what really happened?
9. Explain the subtle changes that take place during the "play extempore."
10. How does Hal manage the sheriff's investigation of the reported robbery?

Answers

1. The conditions that prevail at the inn are such that the "house is turned upside down since Robin Ostler died." The "peas and beans are as dank" as a dog, and the inn is overrun by fleas. This environment reflects the topsy-turvy world of the King's court and state of England. Gadshill among his cronies mirrors the treachery that exists within the King's council.
2. Poins removes Falstaff's horse so he cannot run away after robbing the travelers. Then Hal tells Falstaff to lie down and "lay thine ear close to the ground, and list if thou canst hear the tread of travelers." Poins and Hal arrange to have Falstaff and his gang meet the travelers "in a narrow lane" while Hal and Poins go off to another place with the excuse that if the travelers elude Falstaff they will be sure to meet up with Hal and Poins.
3. Falstaff and his men rob the travelers, bind them, and share the money. Then they are set upon by Hal and Poins. Falstaff is left alone after Bardolph and Peto run away. When he is "attacked" by Hal and Poins, he attempts to defend himself, gets scared, leaves the money, and runs away.
4. Hotspur responds to the letter with disgust because he considers the letter writer "a shallow, cowardly hind...a lack brain...a frosty spirited rogue...such a dish of skim milk." The caution which is suggested in the letter is interpreted as weakness by Hotspur.

5. Lady Percy observes that lately Hotspur has ignored her, lost his appetite, lost his sleep, and seems pensive. She even tells him that in his sleep he speaks "of sallies...trenches...tents... prisoners' ransom" and seems to be at war with something.
6. While Hal waits for Falstaff to return after the robbery, he enlists the aid of Poins to play a practical joke on Francis, the waiter at the inn. In his scheme, he sends Poins off to another part of the inn and instructs him to call Francis while Hal engages Francis in a conversation. The interruptions increase until Francis is torn in two different directions.
7. When Falstaff arrives at the inn, he is exhausted and annoyed at the cowardice of his comrades who deserted him during the "robbery." He is perturbed over the "roguery to be found in villainous man."
8. Falstaff tells his story and exaggerates the number of men who attacked Bardolph, Peto, and him. He also lies about how brutally he was attacked when he points out his ripped shirt, fallen stockings, bent buckler, and dented sword.
9. The "play extempore" begins in the humorous vein with which Falstaff and Hal's relationship was introduced at the

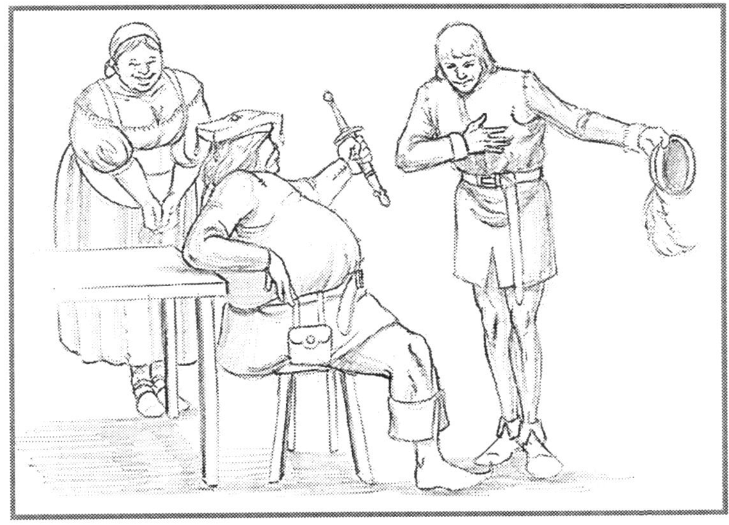

beginning of the play. Falstaff, as King Henry, teases with "that thou art my son I have partly thy mother's word, partly my own opinion." Hal, as himself, mocks Falstaff as "a tun of man." However, they switch parts, and Hal's tone when he calls Falstaff "villainous...in all things," suggests that there is some truth to his accusation. Consequently, Falstaff remarks "I would your Grace would you take me with you." It appears that Falstaff is speaking as himself and not as Hal.

10. To keep Falstaff out of trouble, Hal tells the sheriff that the "gross fat man" is not present and that Hal will "send him to answer thee."

Suggested Essay Topics

1. Explain the comic effects of Falstaff's verbal and physical humor.
2. Analyze the purpose of the "play extempore" in terms of what prompted it to occur, what it reveals about the relationship between Hal and Falstaff, and what serious implications it contains.

SECTION FOUR

Act III

Act III, Scene 1

New Characters:

Lord Mortimer: *Edmund, Earl of March*

Lady Mortimer: *wife to Mortimer; daughter to Glendower*

Owen Glendower: *Welsh rebel; father to Lady Mortimer*

Summary

In Wales, the Percys meet to plan their rebellion and divide the kingdom that they hope to win. Glendower takes this opportunity to talk about how the strange phenomena which occurred at this birth support his claim to magical powers. Hotspur is quick to dismiss these happenings as mere coincidence. The rebels then divide the kingdom, and Hotspur objects that his portion is not equal to the rest. Mortimer and Glendower try to convince Hotspur that his portion is equal, but Hotspur insists he is right. Glendower leaves to inform the men's wives of their departure. When Mortimer asks Hotspur why he is so quick to anger at Glendower, Hotspur says that he is tired of hearing about Glendower's magic. Nevertheless, Worcester instructs Hotspur that he should curb his quick temper. Hotspur brushes Worcester off, and Glendower returns with Lady Mortimer and Lady Percy.

As they say their good-byes, Glendower acts as translator between Lord and Lady Mortimer, since she speaks no English, and

Mortimer, no Welsh. Lady Mortimer sings a Welsh song as they all relax before the men leave for battle.

Analysis

The rebels' plot begins to crystalize as Worcester, Hotspur, Glendower, and Mortimer meet to divide the kingdom, yet they show division among themselves. One weakness among them is Hotspur's attitude toward Glendower, who says that at his "birth / The frame and huge foundation of the earth / Shaked like a coward." Glendower's insistence that supernatural phenomena occurred at his birth finally causes Hotspur to dismiss Glendower as "tedious / As a tired horse." With respect to the division of the kingdom, Hotspur is quick to point out that his share "in quantity equals not" the others' shares, and he disputes with Glendower that the map should be altered. At this point, the seriousness of the rebels' purpose is reduced to a trifling, almost childish, argument in which Glendower insists the map will not be changed and Hotspur insists that he will "cavil on the ninth part of a hair" if he has to in order to make his point. As was evident in a previous scene in which Hotspur could not drop the issue of being silenced about Mortimer, Hotspur does not drop the issue of the size of his portion of the kingdom until he speaks the last word. Worcester points out Hotspur's quickness to assert his willfulness as a fault which he "must needs learn to amend."

As Shakespeare often assigns names to characters that suggest their personality, Hotspur's name suits his character, in that he is like a hot spur which, if jabbed into a horse's side, would cause the horse to take off aimlessly. When he is off in his own direction, Hotspur is not easily led back by those who may be more knowledgeable than he. Even Lady Percy remarks, although in a lighter vein, that Hotspur is "altogether governed by humors," recognizing that he often acts without thinking. The reference to Hotspur's humor points out the Elizabethan belief that four humors or body

fluids, yellow bile, black bile, blood, and phlegm, determine a person's temperament. According to the theory, when all of the body fluids are in equilibrium, a person exhibits balanced behavior. However, if one fluid or a combination dominates, a person exhibits a variety of temperaments and is classified as choleric, melancholy, sanguine, or phlegmatic. Hotspur is indeed motivated by emotions rather than by rational thought.

Act III, Scene 2

Summary

King Henry meets with his son Hal at the palace in London to discuss Hal's friends and the type of behavior he exhibits among them. Hal admits that he acts the way he does because of his youth, and the King lets Hal know that his friends are not the kind among whom he should be seen. He adds that Hal's younger brother, Prince John, has replaced Hal in the council and that Hal has alienated himself from the court. Furthermore, Henry informs Hal that he is ruining his chances of becoming king. Henry uses his own experiences to remind Hal that if he had been loose in his behavior, his own reputation would not have been so good. By likening Hal's behavior to that of Richard II, Henry points out to Hal how unbefitting to a prince his behavior has become. Consequently, Hal promises to change his behavior to suit his regal position, and Henry tells Hal about the seriousness of the Percy Rebellion. As a result, Hal vows to prove himself.

Sir Walter Blunt enters with news that the rebels have met at Shrewsbury. Henry tells Blunt that he has already dispatched the Earl of Westmoreland and Lord John of Lancaster, his younger son. Next, he directs Hal to march next Wednesday so as to meet him at Bridgenorth the following Thursday.

Analysis

This crucial meeting between father and son has been foreshadowed by the "play extempore"; however, there is no comedy as Henry expresses his disappointment in Hal's behavior and the company he keeps. Henry's question to Hal concerns "such poor, such bare, such lewd, such mean attempts, / Such barren pleasure, such rude society" with which he associates himself. Hal admits to his father that he wishes he could clear himself of all of the charges directed at him. On the other hand, for those he does admit to, he judges them as errors of his youth. Henry forgives Hal for the offenses and explains to Hal the consequences of his actions. First, Prince John, Hal's younger brother, has taken Hal's "place in the council." Next, Hal has become "alien to the hearts / Of all the court." As a result, Hal's place as future king of England is in jeopardy. Since Hal is the older son, the throne would naturally go to him, but because of his actions, he is losing the right. Henry advises Hal to keep a low profile and to not be "so common-hackneyed in the eyes of men, / So stale and cheap to vulgar company" so that he may gain public favor when he becomes king.

The next part of Henry's speech to Hal presents the image of Richard II as one who "grew a companion to the common streets" and, as a result, lost his credibility because he was "heard—not regarded." By telling Hal about Richard's errant behavior, Henry hopes to let Hal see that he is following the same path and has already lost his "princely privilege / With vile participation" because of the company he keeps. Hal recognizes what his father says as truth and promises to act as he should. Finally, Henry acknowledges that the situation which exists in England is as it was when Henry seized power from Richard II. His analogy suggests that if nothing is done, Hotspur will seize power sooner than Hal will inherit the crown. After this, Henry gives Hal a detailed description of Hotspur's militant actions and refers to him as "Mars in swathling clothes / This infant warrior." Henry cleverly holds up the warlike image of Hotspur to Hal in order to motivate Hal to action. Consequently, Henry is successful. Hal responds that he "will redeem all this on Percy's head." The word redeem, which was significant to Hotspur in reclaiming his family honor, becomes the motivating force for Hal to maintain his family's reputation. As he rises to the occasion, Hal vows to "make this northern youth exchange / His glorious deeds for my indignities." The scene ends on a note of unity as Henry bestows "charge and soveriegn trust" on his son and explains the strategy for attack.

Act III, Scene 3

Summary

In the Boar's Head Tavern in Eastcheap, Falstaff and Bardolph make an absurd deal in which Falstaff will change his life if Bardolph will change his face. Mistress Quickly enters, and Falstaff asks her if she inquired about who picked his pockets. The hostess is insulted by Falstaff's suggestion that she has thieves for clients, so she calls him to account for the debts he owes.

At this point, the Prince and Poins enter marching, and Falstaff meets them, playing on a large stick as if it were a fife. Falstaff brings up the issue of his being pickpocketed, and after some bantering among them, Hal tells Falstaff that he picked Falstaff's pocket after the sheriff left the inn. Hal also says that the money that Falstaff had stolen from the travelers was paid back and that he has procured for Falstaff a charge of foot soldiers for the ensuing battle. Hal tells Bardolph to deliver a letter to Lord John of Lancaster, Peto to get a horse, and Falstaff to meet him the next day to receive his charge and equipment.

Analysis

Once again, comic relief is used to bridge the gap between dramatic events. This episode at the inn is the last time Hal is seen with his comrades in the common setting, thus implying that Hal's reformation will create a rift in their relationship. Falstaff complains that his "skin hangs about [him] like an old lady's loose gown," suggesting that the incident at Gad's Hill has left its mark on his size. He blames the "company, villainous company" for his transformation. Falstaff says he "swore little, diced not above seven times a week, went to a bawdy house...and paid money...borrowed three or four times," living "virtuous enough." However, he is now "all out of order, out of compass." The pun on the word compass emphasizes Falstaff's wit and prompts Bardolph to joke about Falstaff being "out of all reasonable compass"—in other words, immeasurably fat. With a clever response, Falstaff calls attention to a prominent physical feature of Bardolph's, his nose. Falstaff calls Bardolph "The Knight of the Burning Lamp" and makes a speech in mocking praise of Bardolph's nose. In typical Falstaff fashion, he exaggerates a situation to command an audience of listeners.

Falstaff's suggestion that the clientele of the inn consists of thieves and pickpockets insults Mistress Quickly, so she calls Falstaff to account for all the debts he has incurred at the inn. Falstaff is annoyed at this and says that he had "a seal ring...worth forty marks" pickpocketed, to which the hostess says that she heard Hal say it was only made out of copper. As soon as Falstaff has to account for his actions, he resorts to more humor by teasingly calling Hal a knave.

At this point, Hal and Poins come marching in, and Falstaff joins the merriment by pretending to play a fife. When Falstaff mentions the pickpocketing incident, Hal asks him what was stolen. Again Falstaff exaggerates the worth of what he lost, and Hal points out the true value of the ring. What follows is a name calling match between Falstaff and the hostess, with Hal playing Mistress Quickly's part. As the coup de grâce to this scene, Hal says that Falstaff's pockets contained "tavern reckonings, memorandums of bawdy houses, and one poor penny-worth of sugar." Falstaff is forced to apologize to Mistress Quickly, and Hal tells Falstaff that the stolen "money is paid back again." Falstaff's accounts have been squared away, and he receives "a charge of foot"—that is, he has been given command of an infantry of men to aid in the battle with the Percys.

This scene is the last one set at the inn, and it signals Hal's break from the tavern world as he, too, is called to account and must accept responsibility for his actions.

Study Questions

1. Why have Hotspur, Worcester, Mortimer, and Glendower met in Wales in the opening scene of Act III?
2. Explain the clash of the personalities between Hotspur and Owen Glendower.
3. How does Mortimer attempt to calm Hotspur down?
4. What is the purpose of the scene involving Lady Percy and Lady Mortimer?
5. What does the meeting between King Henry and Hal reveal about their relationship as father and son as well as present king and future king?
6. How does Hal's vow to Henry relate to his soliloquy at the end of Act I, Scene ii?
7. Explain Falstaff's condition at the opening of Scene iii.
8. What is the function of Mistress Quickly?
9. Explain the mood at the tavern at the end of Scene iii.
10. How does Falstaff get involved in Hal's fight with the Percys?

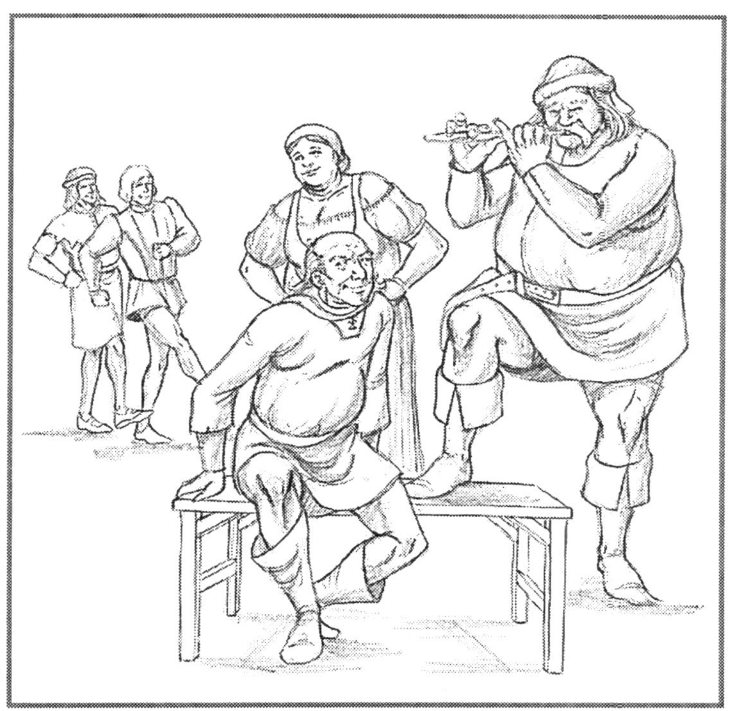

Answers

1. Hotspur, Worcester, Mortimer, and Glendower meet at Bangor, Wales to plan the rebellion and discuss the division of the kingdom that they hope to acquire in the rebellion.

2. Hotspur is annoyed at Glendower's belief that at his "nativity / The front of heaven was full of fiery shapes." Hotspur dismisses these events as mere coincidence. In addition, after the division of the kingdom is made, Hotspur believes his portion is smaller than the rest, so he wants the map altered. Glendower insists it will not be altered, and Hotspur becomes more incensed. Moreover, Hotspur does not care for the "mincing poetry" of Glendower's speech.

3. One of the ways in which Mortimer tries to calm Hotspur down is to present Glendower's admirable qualities such as

his education, valor, and his magical secrets. Mortimer also tells Hotspur that Glendower's patience has been tried many times by Hotspur's mood and temperament.

4. The purpose of the scene between the men and their wives is twofold. First, it provides a moment of calm in the midst of the tension that is brewing. Second, it provides a glimpse of the difference in the relationships that exist between Lord and Lady Mortimer and Hotspur and Lady Percy. Lord Mortimer seems to be a more sensitive, passionate man, whereas Hotspur seems more earthy and less refined as a lover.
5. The meeting between King Henry and Hal reveals that they both have genuine respect for each other. Henry is truly concerned for his son's welfare, and Hal respects his father's position. After Henry expresses his disappointment in Hal's behavior, Hal agrees to amend his conduct to suit his role as Prince of Wales and future King of England.
6. Hal's statement that he "shall hereafter...Be more like" himself parallels his statement in the soliloquy at the end of Act I, Scene ii when he says that like the sun which emerges from behind dark clouds "when he please again to be himself." In the soliloquy, Hal recognizes that he must throw off "this loose behavior" and in this scene, he vows to act.
7. Falstaff pretends that the day's events have made his skin hang about him "like an old lady's gown" and that he is "withered like an old apple-john." As a result, he says that he will repent his former life because "villainous company" has been his ruin.
8. Mistress Quickly provides an excellent foil for Falstaff's rude, insulting, and bawdy remarks because she often misses his intention and creates further occasion for him to taunt her.
9. The mood at the tavern is one of frivolity and laughter as the comrades listen to Falstaff's exaggeration of what was stolen from him, as Falstaff teases Mistress Quickly about the unsafe conditions at the inn, and as Hal and Poins enter marching. The lively atmosphere is subdued as Hal informs

Falstaff of "a charge of foot" which Hal has procured for him as the rebellion becomes a more dominant issue.

10. Falstaff becomes involved after Hal procures an infantry for him and tells Falstaff to meet him "tomorrow in the Temple Hall" in order to "know thy charge."

Suggested Essay Topics

1. Describe the circumstances and conditions that weaken the rebels' cause.
2. Explain how the meeting between Henry and Hal represents the turning point in the play in terms of Hal's rejection of life at the inn and his acceptance of his role in the court.

SECTION FIVE

Act IV

Act IV, Scene 1

New Characters:

Archibald: *Earl of Douglas; captured by Hotspur; member of the rebel faction*

Sir Richard Vernon: *member of the Percy Rebellion*

Messenger: *brings letter from Northumberland to the rebels*

Summary

Hotspur, Worcester, and Douglas meet in the rebel camp near Shrewsbury, and Hotspur tells Douglas what respect he has for him. At this time, a messenger enters with letters from Northumberland informing the rebels that he is sick and will not be able to join the rebellion. Worcester expresses concern that this will weaken the rebels' cause, but Hotspur believes his father's absence will make their plan more daring in the eyes of the opposition. Sir Richard Vernon enters with news that Lord John of Lancaster and the King are marching to Shrewsbury. This news incites Hotspur to battle, and he is eager to meet Hal in a single fight. Vernon adds that Glendower will not be able to join them for another 14 days.

Analysis

In the rebel camp, we see how Hotspur has, as Henry pointed out to Hal, "Discomfited great Douglas; ta'en him once, / Enlarged

him, and made a friend of him," with Hotspur's comment to Douglas, "a braver place / In my heart's love hath no man than yourself." At this, the rebels receive news that Northumberland, who "is grevious sick," will not join them. Worcester fears that Northumberland's "sickness is a maim" to the rebels; however, Hotspur does not perceive it as a weakness. Rather, he is of the opinion that if the rebels' attempts fail, all of their forces will not be destroyed.

Worcester's concern grows as he expresses his belief that others might perceive Northumberland's absence as a sign of his disapproval of the rebels' cause. Hotspur rejects Worcester's ideas and claims that Northumberland's absence "lends a luster and more great opinion, / A larger dare" to their undertaking. This difference of opinion amongst the rebels suggests the dichotomy between Worcester, who is cautious in his approach, and Hotspur, who is quick to act irrationally in spite of many warnings.

Sir Richard Vernon's news that Westmoreland and Prince John with "seven thousand strong" and "the King himself in person" bodes ill for the rebels' cause. When Hotspur mockingly asks where "the nimble-footed madcap Prince of Wales" may be, Vernon says he saw Hal "gallantly armed, / Rise from the ground like feathered Mercury." The mythological allusion to the Roman god parallels Henry's allusion to Hotspur as "Mars in swathling clothes." The allusion is then continued in Hotspur's response that "the mailed Mars shall on his altars sit" as Hotspur prepares the meet "Harry to Harry…hot horse to horse." The mythological allusions elevate

the contest between the rebel forces and the King's forces to a battle of epic proportions between gods.

A final weakness in the rebel enterprise comes with the news that Glendower will not be ready for another 14 days, to which Hotspur responds with the quixotic, "My father and Glendower being both away / The powers of us may serve so great a day." There are logical reasons to delay the battle, but Hotspur disregards them.

Act IV, Scene 2

Summary

On a road near Coventry, Falstaff discusses with Bardolph the ragtag army of men that remain after others he impressed were able to pay their way out of service. The Prince and Westmoreland enter, and Hal tells Falstaff that the men are a pitiful sight. Falstaff remarks that they are as good as any men to serve and be killed.

Analysis

In contrast to a battle of the gods as suggested in the previous scene, Falstaff's army consists of those men who remain after the ones he impressed "bought out their services." Falstaff is disappointed that the men he has enlisted have turned out to be "such toasts and butter" because they paid their way out of service. He is also disgusted with those who are left, whom he describes as "slaves as ragged as Lazarus...discarded serving men...revolted tapsters ...ostlers trade-fall'n; the cankers of a calm world." The biblical allusion, found in Luke 16:19-31, emphasizes the appalling assortment of men who comprise his army. In that parable, Lazarus, a poor man who would have eaten table scraps, is covered with sores which dogs come to lick. Falstaff adds that his army is composed of "a hundred and fifty tattered prodigals lately come from swine keeping." The second allusion to Luke 15:15-16 refers to the Prodigal Son who wasted all his inheritance and had to resort to tending swine to earn a living.

Together, the two allusions create a vivid picture of men who are far removed from the well-trained, well-groomed army of the

King. Falstaff's assessment of his men may, at first, seem to be an exaggeration, since we have seen his bending of the truth in other comic scenes. However, this time his description comes closer to the reality that exists as evinced by Hal's statement that he "did never see such pitiful rascals." Furthermore, Worcester's observation that "they are exceedingly poor and bare, too beggarly," mirrors Falstaff's depiction of the men.

Act IV, Scene 3

Summary

At the rebel camp in Shrewsbury, Worcester and Vernon advise Hotspur and Douglas not to fight this night, but Hotspur and Douglas, eager to fight, disagree with their judgment. Sir Walter Blunt enters with an offer from King Henry. If the rebels name their grievances, the King will see to it that the grievances are met and that the Percys are pardoned for their rebellion. Hotspur gets incensed by this offer and states how the Percys helped Henry regain his position as Duke of Lancaster and how Henry denounced King Richard's abuses and then deposed him. In addition, Hotspur states that taxes are as high now as they were under Richard and that Henry makes no attempt to pay the ransom to get Mortimer released from the Welsh rebels. Hotspur responds to the King's message by telling Blunt that Worcester will come the next day to talk to the King.

Analysis

Again Hotspur displays his irrational thinking as he says "We'll fight with him tonight," despite Worcester's suggestion to "be advised: stir not tonight." Hotspur remains adamant in his belief that the rebels should strike tonight regardless of Vernon's logic that certain forces have not arrived, Worcester's horses are "with hard labor tame and dull," and the number of King's men is greater than the number of rebels. Frustrated because Hotspur will not listen to reason, Worcester admonishes, "For God's sake, cousin, stay till all come in."

At this point, Sir Walter Blunt brings an offer from King Henry

that if the rebels name their griefs they will have their "desires met with interest / And pardon absolute." Hotspur responds by recounting the history of how Henry became king and how the Percys helped. Hotspur's vociferous catalogue of events causes Blunt to sharply reply, "Tut! I came not to hear this." After a long-winded speech which would seem to end in a flat denial of the King's offer, Hotspur reverses his position and tells Blunt that word will be sent in the morning and even suggests an acceptance of Henry's offer. Hotspur's erratic decision-making process suggests that he is inexperienced in war strategy, visualizes war in idealistic images, and refuses to accept the knowledge and insight of others more experienced then he.

Act IV, Scene 4

New Characters:

Archbishop of York: *a member of the Percy conspiracy*

Sir Michael: *the Archbishop of York's friend*

Summary

The Archbishop of York and his friend, Sir Michael, discuss the status of the rebel forces on the eve of the Battle of Shrewsbury. He fears that the absence of Northumberland and Glendower will weaken the rebel forces. Sir Michael tries to assure the Archbishop that the rebels still have Douglas, Mortimer, Mordake, Vernon, Lord Harry Percy, Worcester, and many gallant warriors, but the Archbishop tells him that Mortimer is not with them. The Archbishop also says that the King has drawn up a special army consisting of Hal, Lord John of Lancaster, Westmoreland, Blunt, and many others. Finally, the Archbishop speedily dispatches letters to the Lord Marshall and his cousin Scroop.

Analysis

On the eve of the rebellion, the rebel forces are at a disadvantage as the Archbishop of York fears "the power of Percy is too weak / To wage an instant trial with the King." Even the Archbishop recognizes what Hotspur refuses to accept: that Northumberland's sickness, Glendower's absence, and Mortimer's exclusion severely weaken the rebels' power and diminish their chances of success despite "a head / Of gallant warriors." Moreover, the Archbishop expresses the fear that his own duplicity will be discovered by Henry who "hath heard of our confederacy."

Study Questions

1. What disappointing news do the rebels receive?
2. How does Hotspur react to this news?
3. Why does Worcester fear Northumberland's absence?
4. What news does Sir Richard Vernon bring the rebels?

5. Describe Falstaff's charge of infantry men.
6. What advice do Worcester and Vernon give Hotspur?
7. Explain what Sir Walter Blunt offers the rebels on behalf of King Henry.
8. How does Hotspur respond to the King's proposal?
9. What does the shift in Hotspur's decision suggest about his way of thinking?
10. What fear does the Archbishop of York express?

Answers

1. The rebels receive the disappointing news that Northumberland "is grievous sick" and will not join the rebel forces, that "The Earl of Westmoreland, seven thousand strong, / Is marching," and that Glendower "cannot draw his power this fourteen days."
2. Hotspur reacts to this news by thinking that with Northumberland's absence the rebels will not jeopardize all of their forces. He refuses to comprehend the strength of Henry's forces, and he is naive enough to believe that "the powers of us may serve" to defeat the King.
3. Worcester fears that Northumberland's absence may be interpreted by some as a disapproval of the rebels' cause and may create doubts about their enterprise.
4. Sir Richard Vernon brings news that he saw the King's army "All furnished, all in arms" and Hal "gallantly armed" and ready for battle.
5. Falstaff is left with a ragtag army of men who remain after those he impressed paid their way out of service. Falstaff's army is made up of the dross of society whom he describes as "a hundred and fifty tattered prodigals lately come from swine-keeping, from eating draff and husks." They are a motley collection of runaways and unemployed common men.
6. Worcester advises Hotspur to wait before he fights, and Vernon agrees with Worcester's strategy. Vernon also warns

that certain forces have not yet arrived, the horses are tired, and the number of the King's men exceeds the number of rebels. However, Hotspur does not listen to the advice and maintains his own view of the situation.

7. Sir Walter Blunt brings an offer from the King. If the rebels name their griefs, King Henry will make sure "with all speed" that they "have [their] desires with interest / And pardon absolute" for their transgressions.
8. Hotspur responds to the King's offer by itemizing the events that led up to Henry's rise to power. Blunt stops him with a curt "Tut! I came not to hear this." Again Hotspur continues to list the injuries he feels that the Percys and the kingdom have suffered at the hands of King Henry.
9. After Hotspur tells Blunt that he will send word with his uncle in the morning, Blunt says that he wishes Hotspur would accept the offer. Hotspur responds, "And may be so we shall," a suggestion which contradicts his previous declamations and suggests his inconsistent way of handling matters.
10. The Archbishop of York fears both for his own life since the Percys might not be successful and that his own duplicity will be discovered "For [Henry] hath heard of our confederacy."

Suggested Essay Topics

1. Describe Hotspur's interactions with Worcester, Vernon, and Sir Walter Blunt over the course of Act IV and explain what they reveal about his nature.
2. Explain how the rebels' cause has lost its effectiveness during Act IV.

SECTION SIX

Act V

Act V, Scene 1

Summary

At the King's camp near Shrewsbury, Worcester enters and reminds the King of all the Percys did to ensure Henry's power. The King notes his remarks and tells him that he isn't saying anything that hasn't already been said to give the rebel cause some justification. Hal adds that he will defend his father's position and challenges Hotspur to a single fight. Again, the King makes his offer to the rebels and wants to be sent word about what they decide to do. He strongly suggests that they acquiesce or pay dire consequences.

When Worcester leaves, Hal tells his father that he doesn't believe the rebels will accept the terms. At the end of the scene, Falstaff muses about the value of honor in fighting a battle.

Analysis

The atmosphere in the King's camp the morning of the battle is one which "foretells a tempest and a blustering day." The King notices "How bloodily the sun begins to peer / Above yon bulky hill!" evoking the image of Mars, the Roman god of war, to which Hotspur was compared in a previous scene. The foreboding dawn, one of Shakespeare's stylistic techniques, signals a crucial moment to come in the drama on the battlefield.

When Worcester arrives, he reminds Henry of all that the Percys did to help him gain power. However, Worcester's words have become a cliché to Henry, who is faced with imminent battle. Henry addresses Worcester's comments by telling him that what has been said is a way of distorting "the garment of rebellion / With some fine color that may please the eye / Of fickle changelings and poor discontents" in a feeble attempt so as to give their rebellion more credibility. Hal asserts that many lives hinge on this battle, and he even acknowledges there being no gentleman "more active-valiant or more valiant-young, / More daring or more bold" than Hotspur. Consequently, Hal challenges to let the battle rest "with him in single fight." Henry concurs and once again tells Worcester "so tell your cousin, and bring me word / What he will do," in one more attempt to avert the imminent bloodshed.

The scene ends with Falstaff's speech about honor in light of the upcoming battle. In the form of questions and answers, Falstaff soliloquizes about the nature of honor, which has been the motivating force behind Hotspur. Hotspur believes that it is easy "to pluck bright honor from the pale-faced moon...and pluck up drowned honor by the locks." Hotspur's idealistic view of honor sharply contrasts Falstaff's more realistic conclusion that honor is just a word with no substance because "'tis insensible." The nature of honor also provides a suitable subject for Falstaff's characteristic use of pun. Being insensible, honor can neither be heard nor felt by the dead who have died for it. For the living, honor is merely a coat of arms carried for the dead. Falstaff concludes his "catechism" by declaring, "I'll none of it."

Act V, Scene 2

New Character:

Messenger: *enters with news from the king*

Summary

In the rebel camp near Shrewsbury, Worcester tells Sir Richard Vernon that Hotspur must not know about Henry's offer of pardon, but Vernon thinks Hotspur should know. Worcester believes Henry will not keep his word and will punish the rebels. Hotspur and Douglas enter, and Hotspur releases Westmoreland since Worcester has returned safely. Worcester lies and tells Hotspur that the King will meet him in battle, so Douglas goes after Westmoreland to bring word back to Henry of the rebels' defiance. Worcester adds that Henry called them rebels and traitors and will scourge their name. Douglas reenters and affirms that Westmoreland has delivered the offer which will be met with swiftly. Worcester does, however, tell Hotspur that Hal challenged him to a single fight.

After Hotspur's eager acceptance of the challenge, Vernon says that Hal spoke highly of Hotspur, but Hotspur thinks Vernon is impressed with Hal's reformed behavior. A messenger enters with news that the King is marching toward them as Hotspur prepares to do battle.

Analysis

Worcester believes that Hotspur must not know "the liberal and kind offer of the King" because "it is not possible…the King should keep his word in loving us." Worcester is sure Henry would eventually excuse Hotspur as "hare-brained" and "governed by spleen," but Worcester feels Henry would not be so magnanimous with the other conspirators "as the spring of all." To keep Hotspur in battle, Worcester lies and tells him that Henry "will bid you battle presently." When Hotspur learns that Hal has challenged him to a single fight, he wants to know if the challenge was made with contempt.

Vernon tells Hotspur that he never heard "a challenge urged more modestly" in which Hal "trimmed up [Hotspur's] praises with a princely tongue." Hotspur accuses Vernon of being impressed with Hal's reformation and calls to "Arm with speed." Hotspur is ready to accept Hal's challenge, unaware that Hal has proposed that the single combat determine the outcome of the rebellion.

Act V, Scene 3

Summary

On the battlefield at Shrewsbury, the King enters with his army. Douglas meets Sir Walter Blunt who is disguised as the King. They fight, and Douglas kills Blunt. Hotspur enters and lets Douglas know he killed Blunt, not the true king. He adds that there are many men disguised as Henry; consequently, Douglas vows to kill all of them whom he encounters.

Next, Falstaff enters and stumbles upon Blunt. When Hal enters and asks Falstaff why he is idle, he says that only three of his 150 soldiers are alive. Consequently, Hal asks for Falstaff's sword, but Falstaff offers him a pistol. When the pistol turns out to be a bottle of sack, Hal realizes that Falstaff has been drinking and exits in disgust. This time Falstaff philosophizes about the value of an honorable death in battle.

Analysis

When Douglas meets Blunt on the battlefield, Blunt is disguised as the King. After they fight and Douglas kills him, Hotspur tells Douglas that Blunt was "semblably furnished like the King himself" and that "the King hath many marching in his coats." The disguise suggests the "counterfeit" nature of Henry's position, in that he gained power through insurrection and regicide rather than through inheritance. To the Percys, Henry is not the true King. When Falstaff enters and sees Blunt's body, he comments "There's honor for you!" which supports his previous idea of honor being of no use to a dead man. Hal enters and asks Falstaff why he stands idle, and Falstaff responds that he killed Percy.

In the middle of battle, Falstaff still finds occasion for humor with his use of the word sack. When Hal asks Falstaff for his sword, Falstaff offers his pistol which turns out to be a bottle "that will sack a city." As a pistol, the weapon could destroy a city by killing people; as a bottle of wine, the weapon could wreck a city by causing people to get drunk. In his final examination of honor, Falstaff admits that he does not like "such grinning honor as Sir Walter hath" and makes no attempt to look for a fight in which to engage.

Act V, Scene 4

Summary

On the battlefield at Shrewsbury, the King tells Hal to have his wounds tended to, but Hal refuses to stop fighting. Lord John, Hal's brother, is eager to keep moving forward, and Hal is pleasantly surprised at his eagerness. Next, Douglas enters and meets Henry, whom he thinks is a counterfeit king. Consequently, they fight and Hal intercedes when he sees his father in danger. At this point, Douglas runs away. Hotspur comes on to the field and faces off with Hal, and Hal kills Hotspur.

At the same time in another part of the field, Douglas reenters and fights with Falstaff who feigns death and falls down. After Douglas runs away, Hal sees Falstaff whom he takes for dead. When Hal leaves, Falstaff gets up and sees Hotspur dead. Fearing that Hotspur is faking death too, Falstaff stabs him and carries him on his back. Hal and John enter again and are surprised to see Falstaff alive. At this time, Falstaff takes the opportunity to tell Hal how he and Hotspur had fallen out of breath, got up again, and continued fighting at which time he killed Hotspur.

Analysis

The battle is taking place in various parts of the field as the King's men meet the Percys. King Henry is concerned about Hal who is bleeding, but Hal will not let "a shallow scratch" stop him in action. Lord John of Lancaster is also eager to fight and says, "We breathe too long...our duty lies this way." At this point we see further unity in the family at Hal's recognition of John as "lord of such a spirit" who "lends mettle to us all!" Douglas, thinking he has encountered "another counterfeit" king, enters and remarks to Henry that "thou bearest thee like a king." This statement reflects the Percys' contention that Henry bears the outer trappings of a king but lacks the rightful claim.

As Hal defends his father, Hotspur enters for the final confrontation that has been prepared for in lofty images of war. Both men take a valiant stand. Hal declares that England cannot "brook a double reign of Harry Percy and the Prince of Wales," and Hotspur responds, "Nor shall it Harry, for the hour is come / To end the one of us." Subsequently, Hal fatally wounds Hotspur whose loss of "those proud titles" destroys him more than his mortal wounds. In another part of the battlefield, Falstaff had been fighting Douglas, and Falstaff fell down as if he were dead. Hal sees him and remarks, "O, I should have a heavy miss of thee," in an attempt to cover his sadness by creating a pun with respect to Falstaff's weight. When Falstaff gets up, he justifies his own cowardice by saying, "to counterfeit dying when a man thereby liveth is to be no counterfeit but the true and perfect image of life indeed." For Falstaff, "The better part of valor is discretion," in that valor needs to be regulated by discretion, and for Falstaff discretion means saving one's own life.

In a final comedic act, Falstaff wounds the corpse of Hotspur and carries it upon his back. When Hal enters and sees this, Falstaff lies about how he fought Hotspur and killed him. Hal lets Falstaff off the hook this time by not contradicting him. In fact Hal says, "if a lie may do thee grace / I'll gild it with the happiest terms I have." Hal gives Falstaff a chance to bask in the "honor," however counterfeit it may be.

Act V, Scene 5

Summary

King Henry, the Prince of Wales, Lord John of Lancaster, and Westmoreland enter with Worcester and Vernon as prisoners. The King denounces Worcester for having taken part in the rebellion, and Worcester accepts his fate. Henry orders Vernon and Worcester killed and inquires about the conditions on the field. Hal lets him know that Douglas was taken prisoner after he fled and that Hotspur was slain.

The King lets Hal decide Douglas' fate, so Hal tells his brother John to free Douglas and then determine what his fate will be.

Finally, Henry divides the remaining power. John and Westmoreland are to go to York to meet Northumberland and Scroop, and he and Hal are to go to Wales to meet Glendower and the Earl of March to put an end to more rebellion.

Analysis

The final scene of the play leaves the rebel forces shattered. King Henry reminds "ill-spirited" Worcester of the message wherein he did "send grace, / Pardon and terms of love to all." The King also places the burden on Worcester for not having "truly borne / Betwixt our armies true intelligence." Henry recognizes Worcester's lies and deceit and sentences him to death. Consequently, Worcester accepts his "fortune patiently."

We also learn that Douglas, in one of his attempts to flee, fell down a hill and was captured. Hal asks for the privilege of disposing of Douglas, to which Henry agrees. Hal, in turn, gives John the right to "Go to the Douglas and deliver him / Up to his pleasure." The relegating of power in this action foreshadows Hal's acceptance as the role he will play in the future as king.

In his final speech, Henry divides the remaining power. John and Westmoreland are to take care of Northumberland and the Archbishop of York. He and Hal will march toward Glendower and Mortimer, over whose ransom the Battle of Shrewsbury was fought. The play ends as Henry and his forces set out to subdue the remaining rebels.

Study Questions

1. Why does Worcester go to King Henry?
2. What challenge does Hal present to Worcester?
3. Why does Worcester lie to Hotspur about the King's message?
4. What does Vernon say about Hal's challenge to Hotspur?
5. Explain what happens to Sir Walter Blunt on the battlefield.
6. What comic relief provided by Falstaff appears at the end of Scene iii?
7. What happens when Douglas encounters King Henry on the battlefield?

8. How does Hal live up to his vow to King Henry?
9. What is the outcome of Hal's challenge to Hotspur?
10. What immediate arrangements does Henry make to put an end to rebellion in England?

Answers

1. Worcester goes to King Henry to inform him of the rebels' response to the offer of pardon. Henry takes this opportunity to tell Worcester "'Tis not well / That you and I should meet upon such terms / As we meet now," suggesting the inevitable defeat of the Percys.
2. After hearing Worcester's excuses for justifying the rebellion, Prince Henry challenges Hotspur to do battle "in a single fight" to determine the outcome of the rebellion.

3. When Worcester returns to the Percy camp, he tells Hotspur that the "King will bid you battle presently," in order to stir him to battle since the rebels are weakened and have reached the point of no return. He fears that if Hotspur were to accept the offer, King Henry would pardon "a harebrained Hotspur, governed by spleen," but would not deal so favorably with the other Percys.
4. In telling Hotspur about Hal's challenge, Vernon explains how he never "did hear a challenge urged more modestly" and that Hal "trimmed up [Hotspur's] praises with a princely tongue." This observation causes Hotspur to stir to arms even more enthusiastically.
5. Sir Walter Blunt appears on the battlefield disguised as King Henry. When he confronts Douglas, the two men fight, and Douglas kills Blunt. Hotspur enters and tells him that the "King" was actually Blunt "semblably furnished like the King himself" and that there are "many marching in his coats."
6. When Falstaff stumbles upon the dead Blunt, he has the opportunity to expound upon the value of honor and justify his own cowardice. By nature, Falstaff is quick to run from danger as seen in the robbery scene. Now, on the battlefield he has more at stake as he "fear[s] the shot here." Blunt's corpse is proof enough to Falstaff that life is preferable to "such grinning honor as Sir Walter hath."
7. When Douglas meets King Henry on the battlefield, Douglas believes he has encountered another who "counterfeits the person of the King" and challenges him. They fight when the King identifies himself, and Hal steps in to defend his father.
8. Henry proves to be the kind of son he promised to be when he defends his father from Douglas' attack. He also proves himself in the encounter with Hotspur.
9. When Hotspur and Hal finally meet face to face, they valiantly challenge each other. Hal addresses Hotspur as "a very valiant rebel" and Hotspur responds with "Thy name in arms were not as great as mine!" After they fight, Hal kills Hotspur

who has "lost those proud titles" of honor for which he fought so unrelentlessly.

10. First, King Henry sentences Worcester and Vernon to death for their treason. Second, Henry grants Hal's request to dispose of Douglas, which Hal in turn offers to John. Then he sends John and Westmoreland to York to meet with Northumberland and Scroop so as to suppress them. Finally, he and Hal will go to Wales to fight with Glendower and Mortimer, the Earl of March.

Suggested Essay Topics

1. Describe how Blunt, Hotspur, Worcester, Vernon, and Douglas meet their fates in Act V.
2. Explain how the events in Act V establish order to the world under the reign of King Henry.

SECTION SEVEN

Sample Analytical Paper Topics

The following paper topics are based on the entire play. Following each topic is a thesis and sample outline. Use these as starting points for your paper.

Topic #1

Shakespeare's *Henry IV, Part I* bears the name of the English king who reigns during the historical period in the play; however, it is safe to say that the subject of the play concerns the reformation of Hal, Prince of Wales, as he changes from a carefree, fun-loving man to a responsible individual who is prepared to accept the crown of England. Analyze Hal's reformation as he leaves the world of Falstaff's tavern and enters the world of the court and its responsibilities.

Outline

I. Thesis Statement: *After Hal recognizes his irresponsible behavior as a madcap Prince of Wales, he vows to reform his conduct and accept his responsibilities as future King of England. His attempt at reformation is/is not completely successful.*

II. Act I

   A. Hal and Falstaff engage in humorous conversations, namely about Falstaff's size.

   B. Falstaff suggests that, as king, Hal should establish highwaymen as noble and not criminal.

C. Hal says he will appoint Falstaff executioner of thieves.

D. Poins arranges a practical joke with Hal wherein they will rob Falstaff after Bardolph, Peto, and Falstaff rob some travelers.

E. Hal recognizes the transitory nature of the madcap lifestyle he experiences with his friends at the inn and realizes that he must end it someday.

III. Act II

A. Prince Hal and Poins set up Falstaff for the robbery of the travelers.

B. Falstaff, Peto, and Bardolph rob the travelers.

C. Hal and Poins, disguised as thieves, rob Falstaff and the others.

D. Hal plays a practical joke on Francis, the waiter at the Boar's Head Tavern in Eastcheap.

E. Hal practices a mock conversation between Hotspur and Lady Percy regarding Hotspur's militant attitude.

F. Hal goads Falstaff into telling a tall tale about the robbery of the travelers and Falstaff's subsequent ambush.

G. Hal confronts Falstaff with the truth and exposes Falstaff's exaggeration.

H. Falstaff and Hal engage in a "play extempore" in which they rehearse a conversation Hal may have with his father in the morning.

I. During the play extempore, Falstaff, acting as King Henry, detects that Hal's speeches berating Falstaff may have some serious intent.

J. Hal pickpockets Falstaff after the sheriff leaves.

IV. Act III

A. King Henry meets with Hal to discuss Hal's errant behavior and madcap life.

B. Hal vows to prove himself as Prince of Wales should the occasion arise.

C. Hal and Poins enter the tavern marching, and Falstaff and the others join in on the merriment.

D. Hal forces Falstaff to apologize to Mistress Quickly after Falstaff insults her.

E. Hal procures a charge of foot soldiers for Falstaff as Hal begins to assume his responsibilities in the court.

V. Act IV

A. Hal admits that he has never seen "such pitiful rascals" when he sees Falstaff's charge of infantry men.

B. Hal sends word to Hotspur of a challenge to a single fight to determine the outcome of the rebellion.

VI. Act V

A. Hal enters the battlefield, questions Falstaff's idleness, and asks for his weapon.

B. When Falstaff offers Hal a bottle of sack as his pistol, Hal throws the bottle at him.

C. Hal acknowledges the valor of his brother John.

D. When Hal sees his father in danger while fighting Douglas, he then challenges Douglas.

E. Hal engages in a fight with Hotspur and kills him.

F. Hal asks Henry for permission to dispose of Douglas and then defers the honor of deciding Douglas' fate to his brother John.

G. King Henry divides the remaining power and tells Hal they will proceed together against Glendower and Mortimer.

Topic #2

An England beset by war and rebellion is the backdrop for Shakespeare's *Henry IV, Part I.* The disorder that pervades Henry's kingdom can be seen in the political spheres of the court and in the common world of inns and highway robberies. Trace the details of character action and the situations as they present the disorder within the kingdom and the re-establishment of that disorder.

Outline

I. Thesis Statement: *After Henry's opening speech to his council, the actions of the characters and the situations that arise mirror the chaos of the kingdom and the attempts to re-establish order from that chaos.*

II. Act I

A. King Henry discusses dispatching an army to defend the Holy Land.

B. Rebellion in Wales and Scotland force Henry to cancel the army to the Holy Land.

C. King Henry is disappointed that his son is not involved in the matters of the court as befits his title as Prince.

D. Hal, who is Prince of Wales, spends his time at local taverns with his common friends.

E. Hal becomes involved in a madcap practical joke on Falstaff.

F. Henry is determined to deal more harshly with the rebels who try his patience with "these indignities."

G. The issue of Hotspur's denial of prisoners dominates the council meeting.

H. The Percy Rebellion is an attempt to restore the crown to their line after Richard II was deposed.

III. Act II

A. The tavern at Rochester is "turned upside down since Robin Ostler died."

B. The chamberlain pretends to be shocked when Gadshill asks him to take part in the robbery, yet he filches from the clients at the inn.

C. Falstaff robs a group of travelers and in turn is robbed by Poins and Hal disguised as thieves.

D. In a mock conversation between Hal and King Henry, Falstaff, as king, attempts to set his son's life in order.

IV. Act III

A. As the Percys prepare to divide the kingdom, Hotspur and Glendower disagree over the boundaries of each share, which weakens the rebels unity.

B. Henry meets with Hal in an attempt to straighten out his errant ways.

C. At the Boar's Head Tavern, Falstaff is called to pay his debts and put his accounts in order.

D. The frivolity at the inn is disrupted by serious events in the outside world.

V. Act IV

A. The rebel cause shows signs of deterioration despite all attempts to push forward.

B. Hotspur's irrational thinking is a weakness in the rebels' cause, in that the rebels are not unified enough to fight.

C. Hotspur calls his men to arms despite warnings.

D. Falstaff assembles a group of ragtag infantry men to fight on the side of King Henry.

E. Blunt offers the Percys a peace plan, but they reject it.

F. Hotspur responds to the King's proposal with defiance.

VI. Act V

A. King Henry offers the proposal a second time.

B. Hal challenges Hotspur to a single fight to determine the outcome of the rebellion.

C. Worcester deceives Hotspur.

D. Blunt, defending the kingdom, is killed by Douglas.

E. Hal acknowledges his brother's courage and spirit.

F. Hal meets Hotspur in valiant combat and kills him.

G. King Henry orders that Worcester and Vernon are to be killed.

H. Hal receives permission to dispose of Douglas, and passes Douglas' fate on to John.

I. King Henry divides his powers and his men proceed to stifle more rebellions in unified strength.

Topic #3

The creation of characters who parallel yet contrast each other is often used to suggest themes, clarify major issues, or portray character. This use of the dramatic foil is a technique that Shakespeare incorporates in *Henry IV, Part I* in order to emphasize the chaotic situations that exist in Henry's England. Analyze Shakespeare's use of the dramatic foil in terms of the parallels and contrasts of any one of the following pairs: Hotspur and Hal, Falstaff and Hal, Falstaff and Hotspur, Glendower and Hotspur, King Henry and Falstaff, and King Henry and Hotspur.

Outline

I. Thesis Statement: *In order to emphasize the chaotic conditions that exist in Henry's England, Shakespeare uses foils, characters who parallel yet contrast one another. One such pair is ________.*

II. Hotspur and Hal

A. Both men seek honor for their family names.

B. Both men prepare for single combat with each other.

C. Hotspur acts without thinking; Hal is more circumspect in his approach.

D. Hotspur takes no one's advice; Hal follows military procedure.

III. Falstaff and Hal

A. Both Falstaff and Hal enjoy matching wits with each other.

B. Falstaff talks of reformation; Hal reforms.

C. Both command a position of some authority during the rebellion.

D. Falstaff heads an army of infantry men who are improperly outfitted and inexperienced; Hal commands the King's army consisting of well-armed, well-trained men.

E. Hal's presence increases as the play progresses; Falstaff's diminishes.

F. Falstaff speaks of valor but acts the coward; Hal speaks of valor and demonstrates it.

IV. Falstaff and Hotspur

A. Falstaff is motivated by cowardice; Hotspur is motivated by the struggle to reclaim honor.

B. Falstaff ponders abstract ideas but never acts; Hotspur does not think before he acts irrationally.

C. Falstaff and Hotspur both command a disorganized group of men.

V. Glendower and Hotspur

A. Glendower attributes the occurrence of strange phenomena to his birth; Hotspur dismisses such occurrences as coincidence.

B. Glendower has proven himself in battle; Hotspur is inexperienced.

C. Glendower is educated and studied occult arts; Hotspur is not well educated and dismisses the idea of the supernatural.

VI. King Henry and Falstaff

A. Henry's realm is all of England; Falstaff presides over the world of the tavern.

B. Henry's army is well-trained and well-equipped; Falstaff commands an army of rejects.

C. Henry tries to establish order from chaos; Falstaff creates chaos.

D. Henry represents law and order; Falstaff represents lawlessness.

VII. King Henry and Hotspur

A. Henry seeks to re-establish order by stifling the rebellions; Hotspur seeks to re-establish order by deposing Henry.

B. Henry is experienced in military matters and commands a large army of unified men; Hotspur is inexperienced and commands groups of disorganized rebels.

C. Henry calculates and proceeds with caution; Hotspur acts without thinking.

SECTION EIGHT

Bibliography

Quotations from *Henry IV, Part I* are taken from the following edition:

Wright, Louis B. and Virginia A. Lamar, eds. *Henry IV Part I.* The Folger Library. New York: Washington Square Press, 1960.

Other Sources:

Adams, Joseph Quincy. *A Life of William Shakespeare.* Boston and New York: Houghton Mifflin Co., 1951.

Bradley, A. C. "The Rejection of Falstaff," *Oxford Lectures on Poetry.* London: MacMillan & Co., Ltd., 1959.

Characters of Shakespeare's Plays & Lectures on the English Poets. London: MacMillan and Co., Ltd., 1903.

Scott, Mark, Ed. *Shakespearean Criticism.* Detroit, MI: Gale Research Company Book Tower, 1987.

Shakespeare, The Critical Heritage: 1733-1752. Eds. Brian Vickers, Routledge & Kegan Paul. Vol 3. 1975.

Sherbo, Arthur, ed. *Yale Edition of the Works of Samuel Johnson: Johnson on Shakespeare, The.* Vol VII. Yale University Press, 1968.

Smith, D. Nichol, ed. *Eighteenth Century Essays on Shakespeare.* Second Edition. Oxford: Clarendon Press, 1963.

Speaight, Robert. S*hakespeare on the Stage.* Boston and Toronto: Little, Brown and Company, 1973.

Wilson, J. Dover. *The Fortunes of Falstaff.* Cambridge: University Press, 1943.